Pyrrhonian Buddhism

Pyrrhonian Buddhism reconstructs the path to enlightenment shared both by early Buddhists and the ancient Greek sceptics inspired by Pyrrho of Elis, who may have had extended contacts with Buddhists when he accompanied Alexander the Great to India in the third century BCE.

This volume explores striking parallels between early Buddhism and Pyrrhonian scepticism, suggesting their virtual identity. Both movements saw beliefs—fictions mistaken for truths—as the principal source of human suffering. Both practiced suspension of judgment about beliefs to obtain release from suffering, and to achieve enlightenment, which the Buddhists called bodhi and the Pyrrhonists called ataraxia. And both came to understand the structure of human experience without belief, which the Buddhists called dependent origination and the Pyrrhonists described as phenomenalistic atomism.

This book is intended for the general reader, as well as historians, classicists, Buddhist scholars, philosophers, and practitioners of spiritual techniques.

Adrian Kuzminski is the author of *Pyrrhonism: How the Ancient Greeks Reinvented Buddhism* (2008); *Fixing the System: A History of Populism, Ancient & Modern* (2008); *The Ecology of Money: Debt, Growth, and Sustainability* (2015); and *The Soul* (1994). He is an independent scholar living in upstate New York, USA.

Pyrrhonian Buddhism
A Philosophical Reconstruction

Adrian Kuzminski

LONDON AND NEW YORK

First published 2021
by Routledge
2 Park Square, Milton Park, Abingdon, Oxon OX14 4RN

and by Routledge
52 Vanderbilt Avenue, New York, NY 10017

Routledge is an imprint of the Taylor & Francis Group, an informa business

© 2021 Adrian Kuzminski

The right of Adrian Kuzminski to be identified as author of this work has been asserted by him in accordance with sections 77 and 78 of the Copyright, Designs and Patents Act 1988.

All rights reserved. No part of this book may be reprinted or reproduced or utilised in any form or by any electronic, mechanical, or other means, now known or hereafter invented, including photocopying and recording, or in any information storage or retrieval system, without permission in writing from the publishers.

Trademark notice: Product or corporate names may be trademarks or registered trademarks, and are used only for identification and explanation without intent to infringe.

British Library Cataloguing-in-Publication Data
A catalogue record for this book is available from the British Library

Library of Congress Cataloging-in-Publication Data
A catalog record has been requested for this book

ISBN: 978-0-367-63132-1 (hbk)
ISBN: 978-0-367-63164-2 (pbk)
ISBN: 978-1-003-11237-2 (ebk)

Typeset in Times New Roman
by MPS Limited, Dehradun

To the memory of C. W. "Sandy" Huntington, Jr.,
colleague, critic, friend

Contents

	Preface	viii
1	West meets East	1
2	Diogenes Laertius	21
3	Sextus Empiricus	35
4	Timon and Aulus Gellius	52
5	*Pragmata* and dependent origination	65
6	Emptiness and the suspension of belief	92
7	*Ataraxia* and *Bodhi*	102
	Bibliography	111
	Index	117

Preface

An earlier work of mine—*Pyrrhonism: How the Ancient Greeks Reinvented Buddhism* (2008)—explored a series of parallels between Pyrrhonism and Mādhyamaka Buddhism. I was prompted to undertake the broader comparison of Pyrrhonism and Buddhism advanced in this work as a result of a conference on "Buddhism and Scepticism" in which I participated at the Numata Center for Buddhist Studies at the University of Hamburg in Germany in the fall of 2017.

Some of the issues raised in this work are discussed in my essay, "The Evident and the Non-Evident," published in a volume based on the presentations made at the Numata Center conference. See *Buddhism and Scepticism: Historical, Philosophical, and Comparative Perspectives*, ed. O. Hanner (Hamburg Buddhist Studies 12, Bochem/Freiburg: ProjektVerlag, 2020).

I am grateful to the Numata Center conference and its organizers for stimulating this larger work on Pyrrhonian Buddhism. I would also like to thank the late C. W. Huntington, Jr., of Hartwick College, Oren Hanner of the University of California, Berkeley, and the readers for Routledge Press, including Georgois Halkias of the University of Hong Kong, for their comments on earlier versions of this manuscript. Any remaining errors are my responsibility alone.

1 West meets East

This book is not a conventional scholarly work, though it aspires to standards of scholarly inquiry. Nor is it a popular account reporting on the work of others, though it does some of that, too. It is mainly an essay in comparative philosophy which attempts to synthesize, as accurately as possible, two philosophical traditions with remarkable parallels: early Buddhism and ancient Greek Pyrrhonism. These traditions were widely separated by geography, history, culture, and language, but also directly connected by commerce, war, and personal contacts.

The synthesis presented in what follows is an imaginative reconstruction. It is a *tertium quid*, constructed out of elements common to both Buddhism and Pyrrhonism, using vocabulary from each to illuminate the other. The result is a striking picture, a singular account of human experience into which both movements virtually converge. One of these traditions—Buddhism—is an ancient but very much alive world-historical cultural force, with hundreds of millions of adherents across the globe. The other tradition—Pyrrhonism—disappeared as a living movement with the collapse of the classical Western world, although the arguments of the ancient Pyrrhonists have continued to reverberate deeply within modern Western thought.

The idea of some kind of connection between Pyrrhonism and Buddhism is not a new one. In section 437 of *The Will to Power*, Nietzsche characterizes Pyrrho as "a Buddhist for Greece" (though also calling him a nihilist, suggesting an imperfect understanding of Buddhism).[1] The early twentieth-century Scottish classicist John Burnet suggested that Pyrrho might be understood as a "Buddhist Arhat."[2] Scattered references continued, but it wasn't until Everard Flintoff's provocative 1980 article, "Pyrrho and India,"[3] that the Pyrrhonian-Buddhist connection was brought into sharper focus. His article inspired my own 2008 effort, *Pyrrhonism: How the Ancient*

2   *West meets East*

Greeks Reinvented Buddhism.[4] My focus then was limited by certain features shared by the Pyrrhonian Sextus Empiricus, and early Madhyamaka Buddhists. Those parallels, I found, were quite striking. I summed them up this way:

> ... for Pyrrhonism and the Madhyamaka alike dialectical interrogation ... leads to suspension of judgment about non-evident beliefs (claims, cults, magic, dogmas, miracles, theories, attachment, reifications, essences, forms, absolutes, etc.), resulting in a recognition of the "dependent origination," or "emptiness" or "relativity" of the evident (the phenomena, that is, thoughts and sensations as we actually experience them, or reasonably expect to), leading to peace, tranquility, *bodhi*, liberation, awakening.[5]

By Buddhism, I mean a series of unusual accounts of human experience attributed mainly to the Buddha, the earliest principal written evidence of which (the *Tripitaka*, or "three baskets") is found mainly in the Pali *Nikayas* and corresponding Chinese translations, the *Agamas*—material compiled some centuries after the Buddha's lifetime. According to one scholar, Rupert Gethin, "... these texts above all constitute the common ancient heritage of Buddhism."[6] These early accounts, traditionally put under the *hīnayāna* rubric, were in time supplemented by the *māhāyana* literature associated with Madhyamaka and Yogacara. These later texts, insofar as they can be seen to bring out the logical implications of the earlier accounts, can be understood to offer a fuller description of what Buddhists say we actually experience.

Pyrrhonism is far less known than Buddhism. Its founder was Pyrrho (c. 360–270 CE) of Elis (*Ilida*), the ancient Greek city in the Peloponnese, famous for its long, successful management of the Olympic games. Pyrrho accompanied Alexander the Great on his conquests in Asia in the fourth century BCE, and returned to Greece to live a long life as an acknowledged wise man. His disciples accepted, developed, and perpetuated his philosophical practices, establishing a tradition which lasted for 500 years or more, at least until the second or third centuries CE.

The continuity of ancient Pyrrhonism as a living movement is unclear, but on the strength of its surviving texts it seems considerably more likely than not that it was reliably passed on by ongoing networks of thinkers and practitioners, even if they cannot all be confirmed in the meagre historical record left to us. The major surviving Pyrrhonian texts from antiquity to be considered in this work are the biography of Pyrrho by Diogenes Laertius, the multi-volume works of the Pyrrhonian philosopher, Sextus Empiricus, a lengthy fragment by Pyrrho's immediate disciple, Timon of Phlius—the so-called 'Aristocles passage'—and a short essay by the Roman writer, Aulus Gellius. The works of Sextus, Diogenes, and Gellius in particular—from the second and third centuries CE—testify to a distinct, well-documented, and highly developed philosophical movement in Western antiquity that vigorously and thoroughly engaged the other philosophical schools of the day. Timon's fragment offers a concise summary account of Pyrrhonism dating to the very beginning of the tradition.

The common description of experience which emerges in both Pyrrhonian and early Buddhist texts starts with our immediate sensations and thoughts. It directs our attention to how our experience of thoughts and sensations is distorted by various unsubstantiated beliefs most of us hold about them. Our beliefs about the world we experience are the principal sources of human suffering in both traditions. Both developed practices aimed at suspending our beliefs, and thereby alleviating the suffering they cause. This suspension of belief turned out, for both Buddhism and Pyrrhonism, to be the precondition of peace of mind, or what they variously called enlightenment or *bodhi*, and tranquility or *ataraxia*. It was Pyrrho who first introduced both a phenomenalistic ontology and a notion of a state of tranquility, or *ataraxia*, into Greek philosophy. Neither of these were to be found among the Greeks before him, but they were highly likely present at that time among early Buddhists in India.[7]

Articulating the philosophical parallels between Pyrrhonism and Buddhism—particularly their common description of experience—is the main subject of this work. An understanding of Buddhism through Pyrrhonian eyes has significant implications for the philosophical and religious principles held by Buddhists to this very day. At the same time, putting Pyrrhonism in a Buddhist setting brings out a new understanding of the ancient Greek philosophical school, which unfortunately remains little known today, even among educated people. What emerges from this effort at a *tertium quid* is a philosophical construct, a working hypothesis, which I call *Pyrrhonian Buddhism*, an attempt at a synthesis of the two movements.

Pyrrho's encounter with holy men in India was reported, even in antiquity, to have been what inspired his new philosophy. The key testimony for this comes from Diogenes Laertius, writing centuries later, but with access to older texts no longer extant. Pyrrho, Diogenes tells us, "foregathered with the Indian Gymnosophists and with the Magi. This led him to adopt a most noble philosophy."[8] Definitive proof or disproof that Buddhists were included among the *gymnosophists* and *magi* Pyrrho met, or that they specifically led him to his "noble philosophy," is lacking. On that point, we must suspend judgment. Nonetheless, contact between Pyrrho and early Buddhists in India not only cannot be ruled out, but looks to have been likely.

Ancient cross-cultural connections among Greeks and Asians should hardly be surprising, and have in fact been well documented.[9] From the time Cyrus the Great conquered the Ionian Greek city-states of Asia Minor in the middle of the sixth century BCE, many Greeks found themselves part of a vast Persian Empire stretching from the Aegean coast to the Indus Valley. There is testimony in the ancient sources that both Pythagoras and Democritus journeyed perhaps as far as India, or at least to parts of central Asia, where they were able to consult with Indian holy men, commonly called *gymnosophists* by the Greeks, literally naked sophists, or naked wise or learned men. Darius I sent the Greek Scylax to explore the Indus valley, what we now call the Persian gulf, and perhaps other regions, in 517 BCE. Scylax's account in Greek was widely circulated in the West. The Milesian Hecataeus' map of the world in the sixth century BCE included the Indus River, accurately rendered. The Persians knew the Ionian Greeks as Yavanas or Yonas. Other eminent Greeks such as Solon, Lycurgus, Eudoxus, and Cleobulus are reported to have traveled widely in the Persian Empire and interacted with various priests, magi, and wise men.

All that, however, was but prelude to the conquests of Alexander the Great, which swept away the last political barriers to commercial and cultural exchanges between East and West. Alexander and his entourage, including the philosophers Anaxarchus, Callisthenes, and Onesicritus, along with Pyrrho, spent nearly three years in what's now Afghanistan, Pakistan, and northwest India. The best documented encounters with *gymnosophists* occurred in Taxila, where they spent several weeks.[10] It is there that we might plausibly imagine Pyrrho having had his famous encounter, discovering a "most noble philosophy."

My 2008 work, *Pyrrhonism: How the Ancient Greeks Reinvented Buddhism*, was the first book-length attempt in English, as far as I am aware, to assess the parallels between the two traditions. Since then, three scholars in particular—Georgios Halkias, Matthew Neale, and Christopher Beckwith—have made stimulating if debatable contributions to our understanding of this convergence of Pyrrhonism and Buddhism.

Georgios T. Halkias, in two articles, "The Self-Immolation of Kalanos" and "When the Greeks Converted the Buddha," makes perhaps the strongest case yet that the "holy men" Pyrrho met in India were Buddhists. Halkias reminds us that Alexander and his philosophical entourage spent two or more years in Central Asia and western India, including Taxila in Gandhara. He argues that encounters by Alexander and his court with Indian sages—the "naked philosophers" or *gymnosophists*—were not incidental but deliberate and sustained. Greek accounts tell of two groups of *gymnosophists*: the *brahmanas* and the *sramanas*. The *brahmanas* were early brahmins, but Halkias argues persuasively that the *sramanas* were early Buddhists.

We know the *sramanas* were wanderers, or itinerants, who rejected the Vedic orthodoxy of the brahmans. They struggled to make sense of the new doctrines of karma and rebirth, and to free themselves from the cycles of pleasures and pains. The sanskrit *sarmana* has the root of seeker or ascetic, someone who doubts conventional wisdom. Halkias argues that the *sramanas*, unlike Brahmins or Jains or other sects out of India at the time (sceptics, materialists, etc.), exhibited a number of key Buddhist traits. Early Buddhism, he points out, included not only monks living in communal or monastic settings, as subsequently became common, but also these independent, individual wanderers, haunters of the forests and cemeteries, among whom were included "saints and irregulars."

In Halkias' narrative, the *sramanas* practiced a kind of personalized, non-institutionalized Buddhism, far different from the communal, ritualized life of monks in the *sanghas*.[11] The *sramanas* were wandering ascetics committed to personal self-transformation, and also, Halkias notes, to the study of the "nature of things." They exhibited high levels of physical self-control and fortitude, included women in their number, and practiced self-immolation, which he argues was a peculiarly Buddhist trait under certain circumstances. They held out the promise of some kind of liberation from suffering. This is a picture, Halkias argues persuasively, of early Buddhists. One *sramana* in particular, whom the Greeks called Kalanos, accepted residence at Alexander's court, persuaded him to support his family, and accompanied the court from India back to Persia. His extended presence at court among Alexander's philosophers and companions testifies to a sustained level of contact with Indian wise men who may have been Buddhists.

Far from being an isolated event, the evidence Halkias marshalls suggests serious, prolonged exchanges between both sides. It's worth noting that this was also a time of Buddhist missionary zeal and outreach in central Asia, and in Taxila in particular—itself an invitation to engagement. On the Greek side, Alexander's openness—his multiculturalism and religious curiosity—is well documented. Both groups, it is clear, were reaching out. It was Alexander who proposed, and possibly carried out, a marriage of 10,000 men of his Greek army to 10,000 non-Greek, local women. And it was Alexander who directed one of his philosophers, Onesicritus, to investigate the *sramanas* in Taxila and develop contacts with them.

The evidence from Halkias may yet be challenged. But he's established something important: that Buddhist *sramanas* were as likely as anyone else, and perhaps more so, to have been among the *gymnosophists* who inspired in Pyrrho his "most noble philosophy," as his ancient biographer Diogenes Laertius put it. The idea of a decisive Buddhist influence on Pyrrho, and on the movement which followed him, is at least as reasonable as any other hypothesis given the overall evidence of cultural interaction. The young Greek philosopher, in this setting, could well have absorbed the essentials of what the Buddhists had to offer, and transformed them into a Greek medium and idiom. Halkias fleshes-out a possible historical context that makes such Greek-Buddhist exchanges look not only plausible, but likely.

Another scholar, the late Matthew Neale, in his Oxford dissertation *Madhyamaka and Pyrrhonism*,[12] offers an unparalleled detailed assessment of comparable terms and arguments used in common by both Pyrrhonists and Buddhists. Neale's comparative focus is on the Madhyamaka, as a stand-in for Buddhism as a whole, and Sextus Empiricus, as a stand-in for Pyrrhonism as a whole. He compares what he calls the "self-characterization of the two projects"[13] in terms of "doctrinal, historical and linguistic parallels and interactions," supplemented by comparisons of the common critiques both use against their opponents. His largely quantitative conclusions support a close overlap, if not a complete convergence, of the traditions in the material he reviews.

He reports, for instance, that of the 33 ways he has identified in which "the projects characterize themselves," only two (minor points) seem at odds, while 15 other points of self-characterization appear "quite similar ... but with minor differences," and a final 15 appear "closely equivalent." Neale concludes that "the two sides would largely accept each other as undertaking the same project."[14] A similar preponderance of evidence is cited in his comparison of the arguments employed by each school to support a very strong convergence of the two schools. "We can tentatively conclude," he finally remarks, "that these projects do seem to have reached a very similar, and remarkably counter-intuitive, kind of insight about the phenomena of our experience, so similar and with such similar supporting arguments on this topic that one suspects them of at least in part deriving from a common source or even one from the other...."[15]

Unfortunately, Neale develops his comparison of Pyrrhonism and Buddhism relying on three rubrics presumed by most dogmatic Greek philosophy—the logical, the physical, and the ethical. Neale takes the Buddhist Three Doors of Liberation—which he reformulates as signlessness, emptiness, and wishlessness—to be equivalent to the dogmatic Greek categories. This scheme gives him a neat structure to organize his many comparative points, but that structure says far more about dogmatic Greek philosophy than either Pyrrhonism or Buddhism. It is not a scheme central to the architecture of either Pyrrhonism or Buddhism. As a result, the parallels Neale draws, though remarkable in themselves, and a goldmine of information, remain largely unintegrated insofar as he presents no comprehensive structure unique to Buddhism and Pyrrhonism in which to place his findings.

Finally, another recent work, Christopher Beckwith's provocative book, *Greek Buddha: Pyrrho's Encounter with Early Buddhism*, also takes up the issue of Greek-Indian contacts. Beckwith argues that Pyrrho was a Greek Buddhist, perhaps the first one, and that Greek Pyrrhonian texts, surprisingly, may be the earliest reliable evidence we have of Buddhism. In making his case, he advances a number of audacious claims which challenge decades of scholarship. First, Beckwith claims that the earliest reliable, datable form of Buddhism is a Pyrrhonian fragment by Pyrrho's principal disciple, Timon, which he claims offers compelling evidence of what early Buddhism actually was. Second, that what Beckwith calls "normative" Buddhism—that is, Buddhism as we know it, informed by the Pali Canon and other traditional sources, and carried on subsequently in Tibet, China, Japan, and southeast Asia—emerges only in the first century CE, long after the Buddha's lifetime. Third, that the Buddha was reacting mainly against Zoroastrian ideas from central Asia, not Brahmanic ideas from India. And fourth, that the Buddha was a Scythian, not an Indian, and that he lived much later than commonly thought, most likely into the later fifth century BCE. Beckwith argues that the epithet of the Buddha—*Sakyamuni*—means "sage of the Scythians," or Sakas.

Beckwith claims to reach these startling conclusions by disallowing speculation in favor of datable facts. "My approach in this book," he tells us, "is to base all of my main arguments on hard data—inscriptions, datable manuscripts, other dated texts, and archaeological reports. I do not allow traditional belief to determine anything in the book ...." He is concerned, he adds, "only with issues of historical accuracy."[16] Beckwith cites evidence questioning the authenticity of the stone inscriptions of the Mauryan period traditionally attributed to Asoka. He notes the disputed meaning of key terms, such as *dukkha*. For these and other reasons the assumptions of "normative Buddhism"—including monastic life, the veneration of the Buddha, the contemporaneous existence of Jains and Ajivikas in the Buddha's day, the *Pali* canon, the *Abhidharma*, and other later Madhyamaka and Yogacara texts, etc.—cannot, in Beckwith's view, be legitimately superimposed back onto the period of early Buddhism.

What can be attested to the Buddha's lifetime, he maintains, is the introduction of Zoroastrian beliefs under Persian rule into eastern Scythia and what is now north-western India. These views introduced a supreme God, a strict dichotomy between good and evil, and a final judgment after death leading to heaven or hell. It is these "metaphysical" beliefs, Beckwith contends, against which the Buddha reacted, and not those, as commonly supposed, of a Brahmanical tradition for which Beckwith maintains no early evidence exists. His critics, however, including this author, have pushed back strongly against most of his challenging claims, and particularly over his view of what does and does not count as historical evidence.[17]

Whatever the merits of Beckwith's historical claims, the picture he paints of "Pyrrho's Thought," as his opening chapter is entitled, is more problematic. Relying on what's probably the best single piece of evidence of early Pyrrhonism, the Aristocles passage, Beckwith wrestles with what Timon says Pyrrho reports there to have said about *pragmata*, about what they are, what attitude to adopt towards them, and what the outcome of such an attitude would be. Beckwith insists that "the ethical meaning of the word pragmata is absolutely clear,"[18] and proceeds to interpret the passage, and Pyrrho's entire philosophy, as an exercise in ethics.

Beckwith's case depends on a rather tortured reading of the definition of *pragmata* offered in Liddell, Scott, and Jones' *Greek-English Lexicon* [LSJ]. He writes that "the sense 'thing, concrete reality' listed in the LSJ does *not* in fact refer to 'concrete physical things' at all, as one should expect, but only to abstract 'subjects' or 'objects.'"[19] Beckwith offers no evidence which would rule out the plain meaning of *pragmata*, even if other meanings having to do with human states of affairs, circumstances, etc., are recognized as well. Instead, he falls into the Western philosophical prejudice that any entity can be understood only as an abstraction of some sort.

In the Aristocles passage, Timon reports that, according to Pyrrho, *pragmata* have three traits: they are undifferentiated (*adiaphora*), not measurable (*astathmeta*), and undecidable (*anepikrita*). Beckwith proposes to correlate these with the "*Trilaksana*, the 'Three Characteristics' of all *dharmas*, which are *anitya*, or impermanence, *duhkha*, or dissatisfaction, and *anatman*, or no-self." It is odd that Beckwith, who dismisses the 'normative' Buddhism found in the classic texts, nonetheless uncritically embraces the 'normative' formula of the *Trilaksana*. 'All *dharmas*' would also seem to include all the elements of experience, and not just those of ethical matters.

As I hope to show, there is no reason to preclude Pyrrho (or the Buddha) from casting the widest of all nets, one in which all experiences, not just ethical issues, are somehow seen for what they truly are. Beckwith, like Neale, imposes an arbitrary and limiting structure on the scope of Pyrrhonian Buddhism. His ethical focus obscures the deep phenomenalistic ontology—including dependent origination and emptiness—which I hope to show is the distinguishing feature of Pyrrhonian Buddhism.

In sum, Halkias has not proven conclusively that *sramanas* were Buddhists, Neale has not shown that Buddhism and Pyrrhonism are necessarily organized around the traditional tri-part structure of Greek philosophy, and Beckwith has not proven that the Buddha was a Scythian, nor that normative Buddhism was not present much earlier, nor that the Buddha was responding to Zoroastrian beliefs, nor that the Aristocles passage can be read as the *Trilaksana*, and so on.

What they and others (McEvelley, Stoneman) have done is increase the plausibility of broader claims linking the two traditions. It is now clear that Pyrrho spent months if not years in Taxila and Northwest India, at a time when Buddhists were active there. He would have had ample opportunity, it seems, to converse with local *gymnosophists*, whoever they may have been. That *sramanas* were Buddhists is a strong hypothesis, perhaps the best available. The question of direct influence cannot be confirmed with what we know now, yet we remain emboldened to historically imagine what Pyrrho might have learned from early Buddhists given his Greek background. Let us next turn to Pyrrho's Greek antecedents.

Pyrrho, as we're already quoted Diogenes telling us, "foregathered with the Indian Gymnosophists and with the Magi. This led him to adopt a most noble philosophy." There is no particular reason to doubt this strong claim of his. Diogenes is hardly a perfect doxographer, but his *Lives* overall remains a reasonably reliable source, and he had access to numerous texts no longer extant for us, and perhaps even to some of the living Pyrrhonists of his day. His statement about Pyrrho and India is explicit and pointed, but, since it stands alone in the literature, Western classicists and other scholars have been left free to downplay if not ignore it. They have sought, not unreasonably, to find the antecedents of Pyrrho's thinking in his immediate Greek background, especially in his connection with the Democritean, as well as the Megarian, Cynic, and Cyrenaic traditions.

Pyrrho's early mentor, after all, as Diogenes tells us, was Anaxarchus, a known Democritean philosopher, while Megarian philosophers were known to be active in Pyrrho's hometown, Elis. The Megarians, Stilpo and Bryson, are also associated by Diogenes with Pyrrho, and one of his fellow philosophers in Alexander's entourage was the Cynic, Onesicritus, who Pyrrho no doubt knew well. The Cyreniaics as well developed a phenomenalism similar to that found in Pyrrhonism. There have been numerous attempts to understand Pyrrho and Pyrrhonism as somehow constructed out of these more or less indigenous Greek traditions, with outside influences, especially from the East and India, often discounted if not ignored.

One scholar, Kristian Urstad, invokes the Cyrenaics, a school founded by Aristippus, a disciple of Socrates, as a plausible source for Pyrrho's philosophy. While Socrates held virtue to be the greatest good, the Cyrenaics proposed instead that it was pleasure, anticipating the Epicureans. The Cyrenaics made phenomena, particularly the dynamic of pleasure and pain that phenomena present, as the standard for conduct well before the Pyrrhonists, who, it is suggested, could have adopted it from them. Urstad puts it this way: "... both Pyrrhonists and Cyrenaics did not distrust, but accepted and embraced, our immediately evident sensations and thoughts. And both took appearances as their criteria for action, reacting spontaneously and appropriately to the stimulus offered by them."[20]

The Megarians were another Socratic school said to influence Pyrrho. Founded by a different disciple of Socrates', Euclid, they were famous for developing the Socratic style of argumentation, or dialectic, by opposing judgments to one another, just as the Pyrrhonists later did. In his short life of the Stilpo, the Megarian, another philosophical celebrity of the time, Diogenes tells us: "... so far did he excell all the rest in inventiveness and sophistry," he says, "that nearly the whole of Greece was attracted to him and joined the school of Megara."[21] Indeed, Diogenes notes, "It is said that at Athens he so attracted the public that people would run together from the workshops to look at him."[22]

Using his dialectical skills in deploying opposing arguments, Stilpo called into question ideas or concepts said to underlie our more immediate phenomena, much as the Pyrrhonists later did. As Diogenes reports, "... being a consummate master of controversy, he [Stilpo] used to demolish even the ideas, and say that he who asserted the existence of Man meant no individual; he did not mean this man or that. For why should he mean the one more than the other? Therefore neither does he mean this individual man. Again, 'vegetable' is not what is shown to me, for vegetable existed ten thousand years ago. Therefore this is not a vegetable."[23] This demolition of ideas indeed looks a lot like the Pyrrhonian demolition of beliefs.

As far as the Cynics go, another scholar, Richard Bett, notes that "... Pyrrho and the Cynics seem to share a disregard of conventional mores, and of conventional conventions of what things in life are worth striving for; in addition, both Pyrrho and the Cynics seem to have espoused, and to some degree achieved, an exceptional toughness or indifference in the face of life's hardships ...." Bett adds that Pyrrho, like the Cynics, exhibited a "contempt for and withdrawal from almost everything that passed for theoretical enquiry among more conventional thinkers; to this extent he would ... have found the Cynics' attitude agreeable." Bett concludes that "it is highly probable, then, that the Cynics served as an encouragement to certain of the attitudes characteristic of early Pyrrhonism."[24]

Sextus, however, very clearly distinguishes the Cyrenaics from the Pyrrhonists as follows: "Some say that the Cyrenaic persuasion is the same as Scepticism [Pyrrhonism], since it too says that we only apprehend feelings. But it differs from Scepticism since it states that the aim is pleasure and a smooth motion of the flesh, while we say that it is tranquility, which is contrary to the aim they propose—for whether pleasure is present or absent, anyone who affirms that pleasure is the aim submits to troubles .... Further, we suspend judgment (as far as the argument goes) about external existing things, while the Cyrenaics assert that they have an inapprehensible nature."[25] Their recognition of the importance of phenomena is vitiated, according to Sextus, by such dogmatic conclusions.[26]

As for the Megarians, the fusion of the idea of an underlying Parmenidean "One" with the Socratic notion of virtue—for which they were known—would no doubt have struck Pyrrhonists as another dogmatic claim. Stilpo denied that virtue, conceived as a unity across all instances, could be identified with any particular instance of virtue, any more than any particular vegetable or man could be identified with the idea of Vegetable or Man. Stilpo did not yet reach the conclusion, however, to suspend judgment over claims that could not be realized.

He rather suggested the opposite: that the category in question had to be separated and purified, as it were, to be revealed in its essence, apart from its particular instantiations.

The Cynics, in turn, in their refusal to countenance anything other than following the dictates of nature, followed their founder, Antisthenes, another disciple of Socrates, who claimed that a life in accordance with nature was the path to realizing virtue. Subsequent Cynics (Diogenes of Sinope, and Crates the Athenian) gave dramatic, even scandalous displays of living in voluntary poverty and simplicity. But here too we find a fundamental dogmatic claim incompatible with Pyrrhonism: that a simple life, following nature as directly as possible, while eschewing conventions of behavior and morality, as animals do, would produce virtue. The Pyrrhonists did not reject the conventions Cynics deplored, but accepted them; nor did their recognition of the power of natural forces lead them to embrace those forces as vehicles of liberation. In contrast to the Cynics, Pyrrhonists accepted local convention, and learned to endure nature, rather than expecting to be liberated by it.

The most popular Greek candidate as a precedent for Pyrrho, however, has been Democritus. Indeed, the attempt to derive Pyrrhonism from Democritus has been a common strategy among Western scholars, due in part to Pyrrho's association with the Democritean philosopher, Anaxarchus. Perhaps the most emphatic assertion of Democritean sources for Pyrrhonism comes from Thomas McEvilley. There is a certain irony here, given that McEvilley's work, *The Shape of Ancient Thought*—which exhaustively documents a wealth of interactions and parallels between ancient Greeks and Asians before and after Pyrrho—nonetheless insists that there is no serious link between Pyrrhonism and Buddhist thought:

"It is clear," McEvilley asserts, "... that the essentials of Pyrrhonism were already to be found among the followers of Socrates and Democritus in the late fifth and early fourth centuries B. C., well before Alexander's visit to India. If Pyrrhon encountered such doctrines in India, they must simply have reminded him of doctrines that had been common in Greece for a hundred and fifty years and which his own teachers had taught him ...."[27] And which doctrines 'common in Greece for a hundred and fifty years' before Pyrrho does McEvilley have in mind? "... Democritus," he tells us, "had taught the nondifference of phenomena and the eudaimonistic approach to philosophy—philosophy as a path to a tranquil attitude beyond the effect of phenomenal change—which Pyrrhon is sometimes regarded as having received from an Indian teacher."[28]

A more recent expression of this pro-Democritean, anti-Indian view for the source of Pyrrho's inspiration can be found in a joint essay by

Monte Ransome Johnson and Brett Shults: "... altogether," they write, "there is much stronger evidence for an influence of Democritus on Pyrrho than there is for any influence of Buddhists on Pyrrho."[29] What is that evidence? It can be found, Johnson and Shults say, in Democritus' early use of what became the Pyrrhonian mantra of "no more," in the sense of nothing being 'no more this than that.' This was, they point out, a principle of Democritean understanding of phenomena, illustrated in his observation that honey seems sweet to some and bitter to others, and so on—what McEvilley calls the non-difference of phenomena. Democritus seems to have anticipated the relativistic scepticism Pyrrhonists applied to the things, or *pragmata*, we experience. Further, Democritus uses a number of terms (as McEvilley also points out) such as *euthymia*, *athambia*, and even *ataraxia*[30]—all more or less indicating some form of tranquility or freedom from fear, long before the Pyrrhonists (and other Hellenistic schools) took it up.

These arguments, and Pyrrho's connection with the Democritean Anaxarchus, help explain why Pyrrho is reported by Diogenes to have admired Democritus more than any other Greek philosopher. But these and similar examples have to be set against the clear repudiation by Sextus of Democritus as a source of Pyrrhonism. Sextus writes:

> The philosophy of Democritus is also said to have something in common with Scepticism [Pyrrhonism], since it is thought to make use of the same materials as we do. For from the fact that honey appears sweet to some and bitter to others, they say that Democritus deduces that it is neither sweet nor bitter, and for this reason utters the phrase "No more," which is Sceptical. But the Sceptics and Democriteans use the phrase 'No more' in different senses. The latter assign it the sense that neither is the case, we in the sense that we do not know whether some apparent thing is both or neither .... But the clearest distinction is made when Democritus says "In verity there are atoms and void." For by "In verity" he means "In truth"—and I think it is superfluous to remark that he differs from us in saying that atoms and void in truth subsist, even if he does begin from the anomaly in what is apparent.[31]

Democritus, in other words, is clearly labelled a dogmatist by Sextus, no doubt reflecting the final Pyrrhonian attitude towards him, admiration aside.

Moreover, Democritus' own words can be cited to disabuse anyone of any confusion between his views and the Pyrrhonian understanding of experience: "There are two sorts of knowledge," he tells us, "one genuine, one bastard (or *obscure*'). To the latter belong all the following: sight, hearing, smell, taste, touch. The real is separated from this. When the bastard can do no more—neither see more minutely, nor hear, nor smell, nor taste, nor perceive by touch—and a finer investigation is needed, then the genuine comes in as having a tool for distinguishing more finely."[32] No Pyrrhonian, presumably, would make such a dogmatic distinction.

None of these attempts to derive the key aspects of Pyrrhonism from earlier Greek traditions seems convincing. It would be cavalier, however, to dismiss these important Greek precedents to Pyrrhonism as of no consequence. Quite the contrary. The question is not whether Pyrrhonism is essentially a Greek or Indian philosophy. The question is whether Greek and Indian philosophies could actually overlap or even merge, whether aspects of each could find a smooth and harmonious integration with aspects of the other so as to produce a seamless whole. I propose to consider that this is exactly what may have occurred, that Pyrrho's achievement was precisely the creation of such a synthesis—an atomism derived from Democritus with a phenomenalism derived from Buddhism—which we can call Pyrrhonian Buddhism.

Let me suggest how that might have happened. Imagine how Pyrrho, armed as a young man with the atomistic insights of Leucippus, Democritus, and Anaxarchus, might think about the phenomenalism he likely encountered among early Buddhists. For Democritus and his tradition, atoms were believed to be imperceptible, impenetrable particles moving through the void. What Pyrrho might well have done, in trying to understand Buddhism with the mindset of a Greek atomist, is to recognize that the phenomena present to consciousness for Buddhists were in fact the real atoms, very different from the fictional Democritian atoms. In Buddhism, it was not a question of imagined, imperceptible, impenetrable particles moving in the void, as with Democritus, but of actual, perceptible thoughts and sensations moving in the stream of consciousness, endlessly combining and recombining as the facts, or *pragmata*, as Sextus puts it, which we experience. This atomistic phenomenalism is not only to be found in Sextus and later Pyrrhonism, but it seems to be clearly indicated by Pyrrho's immediate disciple, Timon, presumably reflecting Pyrrho himself, in an oft-quoted fragment: "But the apparent is omnipotent wherever it goes."[33]

Atomism can be illustrated using the example of the alphabet—a model invoked by Sextus, and also traceable back to Democritus,[34] and no doubt available to Pyrrho. In any alphabet, the recurring individual letters normally have no linguistic meaning in themselves; they commonly find such meaning only when combined together into words. Although visual and audible letters are consistently correlated, it is only when they are combined with other letters that they are able to display, or represent, a range of thoughts and sensations. Similarly, insofar as phenomena are recognized as recurring elements, or atoms, they too are understood to have no meaning as such, but only when combined with other phenomena to make up our *pragmata*. Like the letters of the alphabet, our phenomenal elements normally do not appear in isolation, but, it seems, only in combinations with one another. A phenomenal element is like a pixel on a computer screen; it displays something only in relation to other pixels. If we try to disassociate a phenomenal element from any other phenomenal element, it disappears, becoming imperceptible.

Phenomenalistic atoms are the immediate thoughts and sensations we experience as directly present to consciousness. They are the thoughts we think, the sights we see, the sounds we hear, the touches we feel, the aromas we smell, and the flavors we taste. They are universals, or recurring qualities, which fluctuate in their impermanence as they appear, disappear, and reappear again, over and over, in a variety of combinations the Greeks called *pragmata*, and we might call the facts of ordinary experience. These *pragmata* appear, disappear, and reappear again, over and over, displaying to consciousness the complex of changing factual relations, sometimes familiar and sometimes novel, which make up our ongoing experience.

Our phenomenalistic atoms, and the arrangements or forms of *pragmata* they display, are intertwined as parts and wholes. Our immediate thoughts and sensations are the atoms of our consciousness, as it were, its smallest parts, insofar as we fail to discern any further parts in their own composition. Similarly, insofar as we fail to discern any further whole to which all the *pragmata* we experience might belong—some further whole into which both our mental and physical experience might be resolved—there too our consciousness necessarily comes to an end.

No other Greek school advanced such a phenomenalistic atomism—a key feature which serves to distinguish Pyrrhonism from its predecessors (and contemporaries). The Democriteans were atomists without being phenomenalists; while the Cyrenaics were phenomenalists without being atomists. All the other Greek schools remained bounded by some implicit if not explicit dogmatic metaphysics which distinguished between appearances (thoughts and sensations) and the conceptual realities which were presumed to inform those appearances, whether or not the determining conceptual realities in question could be observed. The Pyrrhonists stood this dogmatic metaphysics on its head, taking appearances as inescapable facts, while suspending judgment on any possible reality underlying those appearances.

This, I suggest, is the insight that Pyrrho found in his sustained encounters with the *gymnosophists* in India. It is a distinguishing feature of Buddhist philosophy to begin with the flow of experience in consciousness, as opposed to the motion of objects in external space, as the Greeks would have had it. It would have been natural for the young Pyrrho to have translated such a phenomenal approach, insofar as he encountered it among the *sramanas*, into the atomistic thinking he likely brought with him to India. And among the *sramanas*, only Buddhists, it seems, with their recognition of dependent origination, could have presented him with a non-dogmatic phenomenalism congenial to his atomism. They alone could have given him the opportunity to recast dependent origination into atomistic terms—the basis of what I have called the Greek reinvention of Buddhism.[35] Pyrrho's atomism, like the Buddha's, is phenomenalistic, not dogmatic. The elements of the Pyrrhonian-Buddhist phenomenalistic atomism are the immediate thoughts and sensations we directly experience; and it is the combination of these thoughts and sensations which produce the *pragmata*, or facts, of our experience.

A reviewer of my earlier work, M. Jason Reddoch, captures well the larger point I am trying to make: "The key issue," he writes, "is that Pyrrhonism differs from the traditional perspective of Western philosophy in that it does not assume that the physical world requires *some intellectual organizing power* in order to explain it."[36] (My emphasis.) This is an insight, I suggest, Pyrrho would not have found among Democriteans or Cyrenaics or Cynics or anywhere else in Greece, but only among the *gymnosophists* and other *sramanas* in India. And he would not have found it in most of the philosophical schools of India either, which were almost all variously dogmatic. But the one place where he could have found it, where the idea of an "intellectual organizing power" to explain the world is clearly suspended, is in the Buddhist principle of dependent origination. It is distinguished from all other understandings of experience by its explicit denial of any claim to understand the phenomena of experience except in their own terms, as dependently (not independently) arisen.

My goal in this work is to rethink, as fully as possible, the larger philosophical world rooted in phenomenalistic atomism I am calling Pyrrhonian Buddhism. To understand the emergence of phenomenalistic atomism, I suggest that we imagine Pyrrho bringing to India the mind-set of a Democritean atomist, and then imagine him radically transforming the dogmatically postulated, imperceptible atomism of

Democritus by recognizing as atoms the phenomenal, perceptible elements of experience found in the Buddhist doctrine of dependent origination. In making this move, Pyrrho, in effect, replaced the abstract conceptual atomism of the Democriteans with the experiential phenomenalism of the Buddhists. Much of what follows in this work is an explication of phenomenalistic atomism as the natural ontology in which both suffering and liberation occur.

Finally, a word on methodology. Facts, especially historical facts, are normally incomplete, and can be variously rearranged, sometimes in incompatible ways. Consider how our ancestors tried to make sense of the scattered stars of the night sky by imagining lines connecting them, and so constructed constellations in the heavens. But the stars, though fixed for us, can be differently connected, as is evident in the varying projections of the constellations found in different cultures. Another example of struggling with incomplete facts is that of paleontologists comparing fossil fragments. They recognize, however, that different pieces, each a broken part, when combined, contribute to a fuller and more complete picture of a prehistoric creature not otherwise available. It is in a similar sense that we can speak of different readings of more or less the same historical evidence.

When trying to evaluate different proposed relations among some set of fixed facts, we normally employ our historical imagination to sketch out, compare, and reconcile, if we can, the most plausible accounts we have of the various possibilities. This understanding of historical knowledge was developed most acutely by the twentieth-century British philosopher, R. G. Collingwood, most fully in his *Idea of History*. In his view, derived from the eighteenth-century Italian philosopher Giambattista Vico, historical knowledge is an imaginative reconstruction—a literal rethinking— of what most likely happened in the past on the basis of known but often variously or incompletely connected facts. In his 1935 inaugural lecture as Waynflete professor at Oxford, Collingwood put it this way:

> The historians' picture of his subject, whether that subject be a sequence of events or a past state of things, thus appears as a web of imaginative construction stretched between certain fixed points provided by the statements of his authorities; and if these points are frequent enough and the threads spun from each to the next are constructed with due care, always by the *a priori* imagination and never by merely arbitrary fancy, the whole picture is constantly verified by appeal to these data, and runs little risk of losing touch with the reality which it represents.[37]

Collingwood was fond of comparing historical analysis to the work of a detective trying to solve a crime, starting with a few, inconclusive clues. Just as we want to know what happened in a crime scene, so we want to know what happened in an historical event. In both cases, the historical imagination fills in the gaps, and the most plausible account—the "best" story—is the one which accounts for more of the relevant facts than any other. Just as the detective tries to imagine the most compelling picture of the facts, the historian does the same. The dots they connect—the clues—are accepted as facts, unless otherwise demonstrated.

The puzzle isn't usually about the clues as such; it's mostly about how to connect or disconnect them, or, more accurately, what they mean in one set of circumstances vs. another: whether they are relevant or not, whether they should be included or not, and so on. In the case of Pyrrhonism and Buddhism, the clues discussed so far include certain more or less established facts: that considerable contact existed between Greeks and Indians, that Pyrrho met "holy men" in India, that *sramanas* existed, that they likely included Buddhists, that Buddhists were actively proselytizing in central Asia, that Timon's fragment is genuine, etc.

My purpose in this work is to add to these "historical" clues a set of "philosophical" clues. The historical clues we have render conscious exchange of serious philosophical insight between Indians and Greeks not only plausible, but likely, yet they do not establish it. The philosophical clues—features shared perhaps uniquely by Pyrrhonists and Buddhists—bring in another set of facts. These are the facts of phenomenalistic atomism, as I intend to show. Not only do Buddhists and Pyrrhonists both share an atomistic, phenomenalistic ontology, they also hold that that ontology is commonly and widely distorted by the beliefs most of us hold about it, and that these beliefs are the source of our suffering. And they also hold that we can be liberated from these beliefs, and so recover the immediacy of experience in all its tranquility. Disentangling our beliefs from our phenomenal experience is central to both traditions, as we shall see, and testifies, I shall argue, to their virtual identity.

Notes

1 Friedrich Nietzsche, *The Will to Power*, trans. Walter Kaufmann (New York: Vintage Books, 1968), section 437, p. 241.
2 See Georgios T. Halkias, "The Self-Immolation of Kalanos and Other Luminous Encounters among Greeks and Indian Buddhists in the Hellenistic World," *Journal of the Oxford Centre for Buddhist Studies* 8 (Oxford, 2015), 166, n. 8; see also his "When the Greeks Converted the

Buddha: Asymmetrical Transfers of Knowledge in Indo-Greek Cultures," in *Religions and Trade: Religious Formation, Transformation and Cross-Cultural Exchange Between East and West*, ed. Peter Wick and Volker (Leiden: Brill, 2014), 65–115.
3 Everard Flintoff, "Pyrrho and India," *Phronesis* XXV, no. 2 (1980), 88–108.
4 Adrian Kuzminski, *Pyrrhonism: How the Ancient Greeks Reinvented Buddhism* (Lanhan, Lexington Books, 2008).
5 Ibid., 60.
6 Rupert Gethin, quoted in "Agamas" in *The Encyclopedia of Buddhism*, https://encyclopediaofbuddhism.org/wiki/Agamas.
7 See Pascal Massie, "Ataraxia: Tranquility at the End," in *A Companion to Ancient Philosophy*, ed. Sean D Kirkland and Eric Sanday. (Evanston: Northwestern University Press, 2018), 245–262.
8 Diogenes Laertius, *Lives of Eminent Philosophers*, vol. II, trans. R. D. Hicks, (Cambridge: Harvard University Press), 475.
9 See Richard Stoneman, *The Greek Experience of India: From Alexander to the Indo-Greeks* (Princeton, NJ: Princeton University Press, 2019). Stoneman documents a wide range of cultural interactions between the Seleucid empire, the Mauryan empire, and the Indo-Greek kingdoms. See also Thomas McEvilley, *The Shape of Ancient Thought: Comparative Studies in Greek and Indian Philosophies* (New York: Allworth Press, 2002) for a detailed account of interactions between ancient Greeks and Asians.
10 Stoneman, op. cit., chapter 11, "The Indian Philosophers and the Greeks," 289–330.
11 Halkias, "Self-Immolation of Kalanos …," op. cit., 171.
12 Mathew Neale, *Madhyamaka and Pyrrhonism: Doctrinal, Linguistic, and Historical Parallels Between Madhyamaka Buddhism & Hellenic Pyrrhonism* (DPhil diss., Regent's Park College, University of Oxford, 2014).
13 Ibid., vii.
14 Ibid., 44–5.
15 Ibid., 192.
16 Christopher I. Beckwith, *Greek Buddha: Pyrrho's Encounter with Buddhism in Central Asia*, xii–xiii.
17 A discussion of Beckwith's views can be found in the "Comment and Discussion" section of *Philosophy East and West* 68, no. 3, 974–1016, in an exchange of articles by myself, Charles Goodman, and Beckwith. See also: Monte Ransome Johnson and Brett Shults, "Early Pyrrhonism as a Sect of Buddhism? A Case Study in the Methodology of Comparative Philosophy," *Comparative Philosophy* 9, no. 2 (2018), 1–40; see also Stephen Batchelor's review of *Greek Buddha* in *Contemporary Buddhism* 17, no. 1 (2016), 195–215; Johannes Bronkhorst comments on *Greek Buddha* in his *How the Brahmins Won* (Leiden: Brill, 2016), 483–9; and Jerker Blomqvist's review of *Greek Buddha* in the *Bryn Mawr Classical Review* (2016), https://bmcr.brynmawr.edu/2016/2016.02.32/.
18 Beckwith, op. cit., 22.
19 Ibid., 23.
20 Kristian Urstadt, "Review of *Pyrrhonism: How the Ancient Greeks Reinvented Buddhism*," *Journal of Buddhist Ethics* 17 (2010), 65.
21 Laertius, op. cit., vol. 1, Book II, [113], 241/3.

22 Ibid., [119], 247.
23 Ibid., [119], 247.
24 Richard Bett, *Pyrrho: His Antecedents and His Legacy* (Oxford: Oxford University Press, 2000), 164–5.
25 Ibid., [215,] 55.
26 See also Tim O'Keefe, "The Cyrenaics vs. the Pyrrhonists on Knowledge of Appearances," in *New Essays on Ancient Pyrrhonism*, ed. Diego Machuca (Leiden: Brill, 2011), 27–39.
27 Ibid., 495.
28 McEvilley, op. cit., 493.
29 Johnson and Shults, op. cit., 32.
30 Ibid., 34.
31 Sextus Empiricus, *Outlines of Scepticism*, vol. I, trans. Julia Annas and Jonathan Barnes, Cambridge: Cambridge University Press, 1994), [213], 54–5.
32 Kathleen Freeman, *Ancilla to the Pre-Socratic Philosophers: A Complete Translation of the Fragments in Diels, Fragmente der Vorsokratiker* (Cambridge, MA: Harvard University Press, 1966), fragment 11 of Democritus, 93.
33 Laertius, op. cit., Book IX, [105], 517.
34 See Sylvia Berryman, "Democritus," *Stanford Encyclopedia of Philosophy*, revised 2 December 2016, https://plato.stanford.edu/entries/democritus/.
35 Kuzminski, op. cit., *Pyrrhonism*, with the subtitle "How the Ancient Greeks Reinvented Buddhism."
36 M. Jason Reddoch, "Review of *Pyrrhonism: How the Ancient Greeks Reinvented Buddhism*," *Philosophy East and West* 60, no. 3 (July, 2010), 425.
37 Quoted by Fred Inglis, *History Man: The Life of R. G. Collingwood* (Princeton, NJ: Princeton University Press, 2009), 211.

2 Diogenes Laertius

If Pyrrho had extended contacts with Buddhist *sramanas*, if later doctrinal Buddhist statements cannot uncritically be imposed on early Buddhism, if important early evidence of Buddhism may come from Pyrrhonian not Buddhist sources, and if early Buddhism was not a theory of any sort, but a focused practice seeking liberation from disturbance (as was Pyrrhonism), then we can look to the major Pyrrhonian texts for a possible understanding of early Buddhism not otherwise available. These claims are hypothetical, to be sure, and remain open questions. The approach to be pursued here is to put aside issues of historical proof, so far inconclusive, and explore instead the philosophical congruence between what we might plausibly imagine of Pyrrhonian and early Buddhist thought. To this end, we must first clarify what we know of Pyrrhonism, which is far less known, even to educated people, than Buddhism.

There are three major sources in classical antiquity for ancient Pyrrhonism. The earliest is the already mentioned fragment from Timon, Pyrrho's disciple—the so-called "Aristocles passage"—which offers a very brief, highly condensed, but striking summary of Pyrrho's philosophy. The most comprehensive major source of Pyrrhonism is Sextus Empiricus (four volumes in the Loeb classical library), an actual Pyrrhonian practitioner. His *Outlines of Pyrrhonism* gives an extended summary of the ancient school, and his other works offer Pyrrhonian critiques of various ancient Greek philosophical and cultural movements. Sextus had something to say about almost everybody and everything. The third major source, a detailed account of the life of Pyrrho, is the colorful biography by Diogenes Laertius, included in his *Lives of Eminent Philosophers*. An important minor but often overlooked source is the short chapter on Pyrrhonism in the *Attic Nights* of Aulus Gellius. Gellius wrote in the second century CE, around the same time as Sextus and Diogenes, but all of them drew on much earlier sources then still available.[1] Timon, by contrast, a direct disciple of Pyrrho's, stands at the very beginning of the tradition, nearly half a millennium earlier. Yet the continuities are startling, suggesting a distinct movement in thought and practice. We will begin with Diogenes in this chapter, and in subsequent chapters consider Sextus, and then Timon and Gellius

Diogenes was fascinated by Pyrrho, whose biography is perhaps the most intriguing in his series, *Lives of Eminent Philosophers*; but it's not clear how well he understood Pyrrho and his movement.[2] His life of Pyrrho is disjointed, a rather rough, almost scissors-and-paste compilation from a number of sources, some hostile to Pyrrhonism. The text may be corrupt at points. And Diogenes' favorite philosopher, in the end, was Epicurus, not Pyrrho. "Come then," Diogenes writes, concluding his life of Epicurus, the last in his series shortly after Pyrrho, "let me set the seal, so to say, on this philosopher's [Epicurus'] life ... therewith bringing the whole work to a close and making the end of it to coincide with the beginning of happiness."[3] But before taking refuge in Epicurus, Diogenes had a lot to say about Pyrrho and his movement.

Diogenes, in the famous passage right at the beginning of his biography (to quote it more fully) tells us that, during Alexander's expedition, Pyrrho "foregathered with the Indian Gymnosophists and with the Magi. This led him to adopt a most noble philosophy ... taking the form of agnosticism and suspension of judgment. He denied that anything was honorable or dishonourable, just or unjust. And so, universally, he held that there is nothing really existent, but custom and convention govern human action; for no single thing is in itself any more this than that."[4]

As we might expect from a Greek wise man, or yogi, the Pyrrho painted by Diogenes lived a long life as a philosophically independent, eccentric holy man, mostly in his hometown, Elis, in the Peloponnese, far from the intellectual hubbub of Athens—though he was renowned enough to have been given Athenian citizenship. The ancient travel writer, Pausanias, who visited Elis in the second century CE, hundreds of years later, tells us that "in the market ... stands a portrait of Pyrrho, son of Pistokrates, a professional intellectual and a man who never definitely came down on the side of any proposition whatever."[5] Pyrrho, Diogenes tells us, "was so respected by his native city that they made him high priest, and on his account they voted that all philosophers should be exempt from taxation."[6]

Pyrrho, after his return from Alexander's campaigns, "lived in fraternal piety," Diogenes tells us, with his sister, Philista, a midwife.

Diogenes describes his remarkable indifference to circumstances. He was as ready to go to market, wash a pig, "dust the things in the house," or wander the countryside, just as well as to converse with disciples or accept the honors of his city or preside as High Priest—all on an even keel, in tranquility, with each new experience responded to on its own terms. The Buddha too, we might recall, lived similarly at ease, wandering with his followers from place to place, not as a self-punishing ascetic or dogmatizing prophet, but as someone at peace, with the repose of tranquility, as happy with a full stomach as with an empty one, whose liberation was not an escape from the world, but rather, as we shall argue, an ability to incorporate the world into the boundlessness of the indeterminate self.

Diogenes' Pyrrho was also remarkable for his fortitude. "They say," Diogenes relates, "that, when septic salves and surgical and caustic remedies were applied to a wound he had sustained, he did not so much as frown."[7] In another anecdote, Diogenes relates that "when his fellow-passengers on board a ship were all unnerved by a storm, he [Pyrrho] kept calm and confident, pointing to a little pig in the ship that went on eating, and telling them that such was the unperturbed state in which the wise man should keep himself."[8] Further: "And once, when Anaxarchus [his mentor] fell into a slough, he [Pyrrho] passed by without giving him any help, and, while others blamed him, Anaxarchus himself praised his indifference and *sang-froid*."[9]

But this apparent indifference to the varieties of experience should not be confused with passivity. "Once," Diogenes tells us, "he got enraged in his sister's cause ... and he told the man who blamed him that it was not over a weak woman that one should display indifference. When a cur rushed at him and terrified him, he answered his critic that it was not easy entirely to strip oneself of human weakness; but one should strive by all one's might against facts, by deeds if possible, and if not, in word."[10] Diogenes recounts other instances of unusual behavior by Pyrrho, noting that "he was once so angry that he seized the spit with the meat on it and chased his cook right into the marketplace," and on another occasion that "he was so hard pressed by his pupils' questions that he stripped and swam across the Alpheus [river]."[11]

Diogenes does not explain what the point might have been of Pyrrho's chasing his cook or swimming across the river. The episodes are associated with a list of Pyrrho's pupils, including Eurylochus, Hecataeus, Timon, and Nausiphanes. They can be understood, perhaps, even if we don't know the point in question, as dramatic demonstrations to induce insight—just what a Zen master might do to a student. Pyrrho's great reputation in his city and beyond, and his capacity to attract and hold disciples, suggests a method to his madness.

Like any true yogi, Pyrrho apparently achieved a wholesale recalibration of his reactions to his experience. The normal human reactions—to pain, fear, or danger—seemed to be suspended for him, to be sure, but other reactions—to injustice, to threats, to human compassion—seemed to be heightened. As a yogi, or realized being, as Indians might say, Pyrrho would have lived unconventionally by normal standards. Free of the confusions of the erroneous judgments besetting most of us, he would have been able to radically (and appropriately) redistribute his responses to his experiences, thus channeling rather than suppressing or distorting them. This seems to be the person Diogenes is trying to describe. The reader gets the sense that Diogenes is fascinated by, but does not fully understand his larger-than-life subject.

A number of ancient philosophers, including Pythagoras, Empedocles, Apollonius, Socrates, and Plotinus, also fit the bill of a yogi or 'holy man,' as did the Hebrew prophets and John the Baptist and Jesus, and no doubt many others. The similar magical powers and wisdom of Egyptian priests and Babylonian Magi were widely acknowledged. We should include here as well renowned priestesses, such as the Pythia at Delphi, and other 'holy women.' The Eleusinian Mysteries were an accepted ritual for bridging what we would call the secular and sacred worlds. The gods of antiquity did not hesitate to act in the human world, and not least in people's minds. The line between secular and sacred was far more blurred than it is for us. In our time, they are far apart; indeed they are virtual opposites. In the modern prejudice, we associate things secular with what is natural and objective, with evidence and science; and we associate things sacred with what is unnatural and subjective, with ignorance, superstition, and psychological states, rather than divine access or philosophical insight.

What these holy figures, including Pyrrho, had in common is extraordinary behavior, whether understood as self-discipline or self-surrender. They were indifferent to the normal human reactions to events while, at the same time, far from being inactive, they were widely recognized to display a depth of understanding and compassion far beyond the ordinary. Such holy men and women were also credited with embodying the highest ethical values. All of this was revealed, above all, by the eccentric behavior for which they became famous. The very nature of such behavior invites attributions of divine status.

Diogenes quotes a revealing verse of Timon's: "This, Pyrrho, this my heart is fain to know, Whence peace of mind to thee doth freely flow, Why among men thou like a God dost show?"[12]

How did Pyrrho do it? In the Buddhist tradition in India he may well have encountered a very specific practice or technique—meditation—which is almost universally agreed to play a predominant role in the realization of the state of mind exemplified by holy men, that is, liberation followed by the tranquility of enlightenment, or *bodhi*. There is little if any extant evidence that anything like classical Indian techniques of meditation—for example, *vipassana* or *samatha*—were imported at all into the Greco-Roman West, let alone that they were widely practiced there, even though the nature of East-West contact at the time presents that possibility.

Neither Pyrrho nor others in Western antiquity are described as practicing anything as specific as the motionless, sitting posture which has become the standard image of meditation practiced by Indian sects, Buddhists and non-Buddhists alike. What they do display, however, are similar trance-like states of stillness and intense concentration marked by deep preoccupation and withdrawal from ordinary life. In the case of Indian meditative techniques, practiced by Buddhists, Hindus, and others, attention shifts from the external flow of sensations to the internal flow of thoughts, and we see a similar shift, it appears, with the Western holy men. What both traditions seem to share is an intense, observational awareness, marked by external stillness and abiding focus on the flowing of thoughts and sensations in consciousness.

A scholar of early Buddhist meditation, Eviatar Schulman, argues that the trance-states, or *samadi*, culminate in the phenomenal observation of our thoughts in "specific moments of experience." In meditative practice four trace-states, or *jnanas*, are commonly recognized. As Shulman describes it, liberation or enlightenment follows upon an actual conscious perception—specifically occurring in the fourth *jnana*—of how the objects we perceive are in fact related to one another—what he calls "the embodied perception of impermanence." In his view, "the three seminal teachings of Buddhism" [the Four Noble Truths, dependent origination, and selflessness] "all emerge from one, core meditative apprehension regarding the arising and passing away of mental events."[13]

What Schulman calls the embodied perception of impermanence is the realization, in Buddhist language, of dependent origination. In Pyrrhonian language, it's what's left over after the fictional permanent entities (dogmas) we mistakenly posit as the real constituents of our experience are suspended. Suspension of judgment requires close attention to appearances, to the direct observations of thoughts and sensations just as they happen. It is through this specific form of attention that what the Buddhists call dependent origination can be distinguished from interpretation and belief. The systematic listing by Diogenes (and Pyrrhonists like Sextus) of various modes or interpretations of experience, which cancel out one another, parallels the Buddhist meditative review (and subsequent suspension) of all the possibilities which the mind tries to assign to any thought or sensation. In both cases the point is to recognize the mutually conflicting nature of competing interpretations of experience, or beliefs—themselves embodied in certain thoughts—and put them aside, and thereby cease interpreting experience in order to be able instead to see it for what it is in itself. Liberation is liberation from interpretation. This is arguably the practice in which both the Buddha and Pyrrho appear to have been engaged.

It might be noted as well that the *ataraxia* the Pyrrhonists discovered through their atomistic phenomenalism (what's left after suspension of judgment), as reported by Diogenes, is very different from what other Greek philosophers meant by their use of *ataraxia* and related terms such as *euthymia* and *athambia*. Pyrrho is never described as cheerful, like Democritus, nor as a laughing philosopher, like Anaxarchus, nor as a man focused on pleasure and pain, like the Cyrenaics or Epicurus, nor, like the Cynics, a man obsessed with living naturally. Our impression of Pyrrho is rather that of a serene, remarkably self-contained man, indifferent to pleasure and pain, accepting of social convention, not a figure out to lead people or make a name for himself, as with most of the others. The initial impulse of the Buddha after enlightenment was a sense of reticence. His first notion was not to teach his insight, and Pyrrho, perhaps out of the same impulse, was content to live quietly in a repose and tranquility born out of a steady concentration on *pragmata*, and to let others make of his example what they would.

After giving us invaluable biographical information, Diogenes goes on to try to describe the Pyrrhonian movement, its practices, and its critics. The Pyrrhonian philosophers, he says, were called not only Pyrrhonians ("after the name of their master") but Aporetics, Sceptics, Ephectics, and Zetetics. Aporetics were perplexed, Sceptics were inquirers, Ephectics were doubters, and Zetetics were seekers. With these ambiguities in mind, Diogenes favors the term "Sceptics"—in the sense of inquirers—and uses it more or less interchangeably with "Pyrrhonists."

He describes them this way: "The Sceptics [Pyrrhonists] ... were constantly engaged in overthrowing the dogmas of all schools, but enunciated none themselves; and though they would go so far as to bring forward and expound the dogmas of the others, they themselves laid down nothing definitely, not even the laying down of nothing."[14]

In a passage not from his life of Pyrrho but from the Prologue to his *Lives*, Diogenes insightfully describes the Pyrrhonists not as a traditional school but as a movement marked by a peculiar response or "attitude" to appearances: "... as to the Pyrrhonians, so indefinite are their conclusions that hardly any authorities allow them to be a sect.... It would seem, however, that they are a sect, for we use the term of those who in their attitude to appearances follow or seem to follow some principle, and on this ground we should be justified in calling the Sceptics a sect. But if we are to understand by 'sect' a bias in favor of coherent, positive doctrines, they can no longer be called a sect, for they have no positive doctrines."[15]

The principle the Pyrrhonists are said to follow "in their attitude to appearances" is to accept all appearances while suspending all interpretations of appearances. Diogenes elaborates the point, apparently quoting directly from a Pyrrhonist source: "... we recognize that it is day and that we are alive, and many other apparent facts in life; but with regard to the things about which our opponents argue so positively, claiming to have definitely apprehended them, we suspend our judgments because they are not certain, and confine knowledge to our impressions. For we admit that we see, and we recognize that we think this or that, but how we see or how we think we know not. And we say in conversation that a certain thing appears white, but we are not positive that it really is white."

Diogenes continues, in the same passage, still appearing to follow an Pyrrhonian text available to him: "'We admit the apparent fact,' they [the Pyrrhonists] say, 'without admitting that it really is what it appears to be.' We also perceive that fire burns; as to whether it is in its nature to burn, we suspend our judgment. We see that a man moves, and that he perishes; how it happens we do not know. We merely object to accepting the unknown substance behind phenomena."[16]

The claim that there is some "unknown substance behind phenomena," some determinative underlying reality—a form or essence—informing any particular combination of phenomena, or *pragmata*, is mere opinion, Pyrrhonists point out, a speculative fantasy which cannot be established. The "unknown substance" is always over the horizon, always unknown. We imagine that it exists, of course, and that it is there "by nature," just as we can imagine that mermaids, centaurs, unicorns and other creatures also exist "by nature," that is, independently of how they appear in our minds, or in our physical representations (words, pictures, sculptures, etc.) of what appears in our minds. What we imagine in such cases is taken to be not only the immediate mental appearance that it is, but, beyond that, to be a sign of something independently existing apart from how it appears to us.

The independent existence of things like unicorns, or mermaids, Diogenes makes plain, would be established only if we encountered a unicorn, or a mermaid, not only in thought, but also as independently originating in sensation. An independently existing unicorn or mermaid would not be a representation of a thought in sensation, like a picture or model of a unicorn or mermaid we have first imagined, but its appearance, as it were, in sensation independently of whether or not we have ever imagined it. When we cannot find the corresponding independent appearance in sensation of something we imagine in thought—like a unicorn—we can only maintain that the independent realization of a unicorn in sensation is a fact by *believing* it is so. Simply to imagine a thought being a sensation doesn't make it one, even if we believe it to be a sign of such a sensation.

We are entrained (or enthralled, or somehow captivated) in the drama of the sensible, physical world, in which, as the phenomenal stream of our experience passes by, we must take things as they come. But we also have a private theater, as it were, in our minds, where we can imagine a variety of possible things, some of which can be realized in sensation, and others not. Pyrrhonists admit only "the apparent fact," as Diogenes puts it, the immediate sensible or mental phenomenon we can't help but confront. Insofar as an "unknown substance" can be made apparent, therefore, it can be only as a sensible referent which independently corresponds to something we can imagine. It would be as if I actually encountered a unicorn in the forest, and not just imagined doing so. And insofar as we search in vain for any corresponding realization of such an idea, it necessarily remains a belief, a fiction. Lacking such a realization—being "empty," as the Buddhists put it—is precisely the description of apparent phenomenal experience.

Both our sensations and our thoughts (our mental images, or imaginings) are equally apparent to us as the immediate, undeniable objects of consciousness they are. But our sensations are compelling to us in ways that our thoughts are not. They are compelling not only as objects of consciousness, but also as objects of consciousness which persist and recur *whether we like them or not*—like a dream from which we cannot seem to awake. Our thoughts or imaginings, by contrast, can be dismissed in ways that our sensations cannot. A thought may arise spontaneously—an image of a friend, a scene from nature—and we can dismiss it, and let it be replaced by a succeeding thought, or we can persist in attending to it, developing it, etc. But even then, we can usually put it aside if we need or wish to do so. There is a sense in which we can say "no" to mental experience in a way that we cannot say "no" to physical experience, though both are equally realized as appearances.

We awake from our thoughts, it seems, more easily than we awake from our sensations. Sensory experiences are just as involuntarily as our thoughts, but they are structured in ways our thoughts are not. They insist on unfolding themselves in sustained sequences organized into space and time, or *pragmata* ultimately described by the laws of physics. A sensible sequence of events has a structure—a narrative or plot, or causes and effects, or *karma*—that we cannot avoid insofar as we experience sensations. I cannot dismiss my physical sensations—my body in particular and the environment in which it finds itself—the way I can dismiss a sequence of thoughts. The Pyrrhonists make no apologies for this recalcitrance of sensations; we can only learn to endure them, they say, whether painful, pleasurable, or neutral.

Our thoughts, to be sure, though normally free enough, can also get fixed in our minds. It is possible to be obsessed with some mental experience—as demonstrated by classical neurotic or psychotic behavior. But such compulsions too remain subject to choice, at least in principle. When compulsions are forcefully imposed on the mind, say, by a trauma of some kind, the whole aim of therapy, after all, is to reach a point where they can be dismissed by the subject, who is thereby freed of them. There is little point, however, in trying to dismiss the compulsions of the body, without which life itself would be impossible.

These dismissable fixations of thought the Pyrrhonists recognized as beliefs, and the therapy they offered was release from such beliefs. A belief is an assertion we make in thought. It is an interpretation of something in terms of something else; a belief or opinion is a judgment whose referent, or object, is asserted to exist, but (so far) cannot be found. Beliefs or opinions are non-evident judgments. Belief exists only as something we imagine, but, as we've seen, we nonetheless take it to signify a fact existing independently of what we imagine. We can believe that something we imagine can be realized in sensation as well as in thought, even though no realization in sensation may be available to us. We can imagine Zeus and the gods gathering on Mt. Olympus, for instance, even there is no evidence of them ever physically gathering there at any time.

We can also imagine entire worlds—the world of the Harry Potter novels, for instance, or the Middle Earth saga of *The Lord of the Rings*, or any number of parallel imagined universes—but such imaginings are transformed into beliefs only at the point where we take them to also represent sensible facts actually existing somewhere. A dogmatic Christian, for instance, takes the narratives of the four Gospels not simply as something he or she can imagine, but as a series of events which physically occurred in the sensible world in a certain time and place. A dogmatic Marxist similarly takes an image of a post-revolutionary classless society and believes it represents a future state which can be realized in reality.

Furthermore, and crucially, the claim of beliefs to represent not only themselves as imaginative creations, but also to represent independently existing if as yet unverified sensible realities, means they can be contradicted just as easily as they can be asserted. Anyone, given the absence of supporting sensible evidence, can deny the existence of Zeus and the gods at Mt. Olympus. The beliefs or Christians or Marxists or others can be similarly denied. The Pyrrhonian technique for neutralizing beliefs, expressed as opinions, Diogenes tells us, is to pit them against one another in just this way. If the same thing is harmful in one context, for instance, and beneficial in another, then it cannot *in itself* be either harmful or beneficial. This kind of argument is a way of emptying our experience, our thoughts and sensations, of any content other than what is actually present to consciousness. It proceeds by opposing our thoughts and sensations, both each to themselves as well to one another.

The ways in which this can be done were catalogued into so-called "modes" by the Pyrrhonists. Diogenes summarizes the ten modes,[17] also found in Sextus Empiricus—which probably originated with the first century BCE Pyrrhonist, Aenesidemus—as well as the five modes of another obscure Pyrrhonist, Agrippa. The ten modes bring out contradictions among thoughts and sensations with regard to animals, people, sense organs, circumstances, location, composition, quantity, relativity, frequency, and culture. The five modes display contradictions among thoughts and sensations involving disagreement, infinite regress, relativity, hypotheses, and reciprocity. The modes are not fixed rules or rigid logical formulae; nor are they clearly defined. They are rather ad-hoc groupings which sometimes overlap, but they consistently exhibit the emptying of content from various beliefs by contradictory applications of judgment. Several versions of the modes seem to have circulated simultaneously among ancient Pyrrhonists.

The modes demonstrate various conflicting interpretations of appearances which arise when we make judgments about non-evident things. A certain wine, for instance, is said to be tart by some people and smooth by others. But since the wine in question cannot be both tart and smooth, we can only suspend judgment about whether the wine *as such*—the real, underlying wine—is *really* tart or smooth. Or, to take another example, one person may judge that money is good and another that it is evil. But since it cannot in itself be both good and evil, we can only suspend judgment about whether money as such is good or evil.

Some of the modes are more complex than others, some seem trivial and other obscure, but they always involve conflicting interpretations of some non-evident experience created by the competing judgments we make about it. If someone judges, for example, that social justice is "the greatest good for the greatest number," and someone else counters with the denial that "the greatest good is not for the greatest number," the proponent can invoke in defense a further judgment to justify the first one, such as "since people are equal the greater good necessarily includes the greater number." That in turn can elicit a further counter-judgment from the critic, perhaps that "people are not equal," and that in turn a further response from the proponent, and so on endlessly, that is, in the pattern of an infinite regress.

The Pyrrhonian technique or practice evident in all the modes is the neutralization of one belief by another. As a result, Diogenes tells us, "they [the Pyrrhonists] would deny all demonstration, criterion, sign, cause, motion, the process of learning, coming into being, or that there is anything good or bad by nature."[18] That's an astonishing list of beliefs about things for anyone to suspend judgment upon. Nonetheless, Diogenes concludes that, for the Pyrrhonists, *all* judgments which have no phenomenal realization are to be suspended. Diogenes quotes Aenesidemus to the effect "that Pyrrho determines nothing dogmatically, because of the possibility of contradiction, but guides himself by apparent facts."[19] He adds that "the apparent is the Sceptic's criterion, as indeed Aenesidemus says."[20]

The key role of appearances in the Pyrrhonian tradition is evident from Pyrrho through his disciples, including Timon and Aenesidemus, to Sextus, without exception. Once one has suspended beliefs altogether (leaving behind only appearances as the standard of life), a final benefit emerges: a liberation into some kind into tranquility, or peace of mind. As Diogenes puts it: "The end to be realized they [Pyrrhonists or Sceptics] hold to be suspension of judgment, which brings with it tranquility like a shadow."[21]

With the suspension of judgment and liberation from belief, the practitioner, we are told, can see the world as it really is. "The Pyrrhonian principle," as Diogenes puts it, again quoting Aenesidemus, "is but a report on phenomena or on any kind of judgment, a report in which all things are brought to bear on one another, and in the comparison are found to present much anomaly and confusion."[22] A belief is a group of imagined phenomena—say the imagery and narratives we associate with Santa Claus—insofar as it is taken as a sign for something independently existing apart from our imagining it. That would mean Santa Claus really living at the North Pole, really driving a sleigh pulled by real reindeer, really delivering real presents on an actual Christmas eve, and so on. The Pyrrhonian "principle" of phenomenalistic analysis aims to dissolve all such beliefs, whether trivial or profound.

In a concise passage, Diogenes sums up the Pyrrhonian understanding of objects of thought, which leaves no room for signs as conventionally understood. By showing how they dispense with signs, he shows how the Pyrrhonists eliminate the principal mechanism supporting beliefs. They describe objects of thought from a phenomenalistic perspective, solely in terms of what actually appears and what does not appear, which rather astonishingly leads us to suspend judgment about signs altogether:

> "Nor is a sign an object of thought," he tells us, "for objects of thought are of four kinds, apparent judgments on things apparent, non-apparent judgments on things non-apparent, non-apparent on apparent, or apparent on non-apparent; and a sign is none of these, so that there is no such thing as a sign. A sign is not 'apparent' on 'apparent,' for what is apparent needs no sign; nor is it non-apparent on non-apparent, for what is revealed by something must needs appear; nor is it non-apparent on apparent, for that which is to afford the means of apprehending something must itself be apparent; nor, lastly, is it apparent on non-apparent, because the sign, being relative, must be apprehended along with that of which it is the sign, which is not here the case. It follows that nothing uncertain can be apprehended; for it is through signs that uncertain things are said to be apprehended."[23]

Let's try to clarify these subtle and provocative remarks. In the first case, an apparent thought, say an image of a friend, can be correlated with the apparent sight of that friend, in which case the correlation is evident, and requires no separate sign at all. On the other hand, if I have neither an apparent thought nor a correspondingly apparent sensation, it is evident that neither is apparent, and so here too no sign is needed or relevant. Further, if an apparent thought of my friend cannot be correlated with any apparent sight of my friend, it is evident that I have a thought of my friend, but no apparent sight of my friend, so my thought fails to qualify as a sign of my friend as actually existing. (My friend may have died, for instance, leaving me only with thoughts of him or her; but I no longer enjoy any actual experience of my friend as someone apparent to me.) And finally, if I do not have an apparent thought of my friend, who is nonetheless visibly apparent to me—as we see in cases of dementia and other cognitive impairments— then it is evident that I do not recognize a friend even when I actually see them, and so here too the friend I see but cannot think, as it were, is no sign at all.

The non-existence of signs follows from their status as unnecessary fictions. Signs as such turn out to be non-evident, eliciting a suspension of judgment about their independent existence. Our actual experience of phenomena makes plain, Diogenes reports, that we function perfectly well negotiating via our immediate thoughts and sensations without needing to invoke signs at all. The manner in which phenomena are interrelated is sufficient as an account of our experience. Pyrrhonists continue to speak of "signs," as we shall see in the next chapter on Sextus, but only as correlated phenomena and not as independently existing entities. No evident phenomenon is inherently a sign, except in relation to another evident phenomenon, where signification becomes self-evident—at which point the belief in signification evaporates. To believe any phenomenon is inherently a sign is a license to project a fiction. As Diogenes puts it elsewhere, commenting more broadly on appearances and their correlations: "... every phenomenon appears in a certain disposition and in a certain reciprocal relation to surrounding circumstances."[24] Because of this "... a thing can never be apprehended in and by itself, but only in connection with something else."[25]

This is a fundamental point, as we shall see later, made by Buddhists when they invoke dependent origination. Dependent origination is what the Pyrrhonists would call a recognition of actual phenomenal experience, a recognition which can be (and usually is) distorted and denied by beliefs—by things we imagine when we take them as signs, or representatives, of things otherwise non-evident, not apparent. The Sceptic liberated of his or her beliefs, Diogenes tells us, "will be able so to live as to suspend his judgment in cases where it is a question of arriving at the truth, but not in matters of life and the taking of precautions. Accordingly we may choose a thing or shrink from a thing by habit and may observe rules and customs. According to some authorities the end proposed by the Sceptics is insensibility; according to others gentleness."[26]

Notes

1. Another important minor source is the brief passage from the *Library* (169b18–170b35) of Photius summarizing his reading of the lost *Pyrrhonist Discourses* of Aenesidemus, a first century BCE Pyrrhonian; Photius was a ninth-century Byzantine patriarch and scholar and his summary tells us that Aenesidenmus distinguished between Academic and Pyrrhonian philosophers in terms similar to those of later commentators; Aenesidemus' contributions to Pyrrhonism appear to have been largely absorbed by Sextus; for Photius on Aenesidemus, see *The Hellenistic Philosophers*, vol. 1, trans. with commentary by A.A. Long and D.N. Sedley (Cambridge: Cambridge University Press, 1987), see 468–70 and 484–84.
2. For a recent discussion of Diogenes' understanding of Pyrrhonism, see the essays collected in *Pyrrhonian Skepticism in Diogenes Laertius: Introduction, Text, Translation, Commentary and Interpretative Essays*, ed. Katja Maria Vogt (Tubingen: Mohr Siebeck, 2015).
3. Beckwith, op. cit., 663.
4. Laertius, op. cit., vol. II, p. 475.
5. Pausanias, *Guide to Greece*, vol. 2, trans. Peter Levi (New York: Penguin Books, 1971), 359.
6. Laertius, op. cit., 477.
7. Ibid., 479.
8. Ibid., 481.
9. Ibid., 477.
10. Ibid., 479.
11. Ibid., 481–2.
12. Ibid., 479.
13. Eviatar Schulman, *Rethinking the Buddha* (Cambridge: Cambridge University Press, 2014), 189.
14. Ibid., 74, 487.
15. Laertius, op. cit., vol. I, Book 1, [20], 21.
16. Ibid., vol. II, Book 9, [103, 105], 515.
17. Ibid., vols. II, [79–89], 493–501.
18. Ibid., [90], 501.
19. Ibid., [106], 517.
20. Ibid., [106], 517.
21. Ibid., [107], 517/19.
22. Ibid., [78], 491.
23. Ibid., [96–7], 507, 509.
24. Ibid., [92], 503.
25. Ibid., [89], 501.
26. Ibid., [108], 519.

3 Sextus Empiricus

Diogenes' life of Pyrrho is a teaser, a combination of colorful vignettes with somewhat cryptic summaries of Pyrrhonian philosophy and practices. We're left with an idea of Pyrrhonism as a philosophical practice inspired by Indian *gymnosophists* and marked by (1) a reliance on appearances, including custom and convention, as the basis of experience, (2) suspension of judgment over objects asserted by beliefs (*dogmas*), and (3) the discovery of tranquility (*ataraxia*) as a result. We find the same points in Buddhist texts: a focus on appearances, suspension of judgment about speculative matters (beliefs), and a promise of liberation, or *nirvana*,[1] into tranquility, *ataraxia* or *bodhi*. Let us further develop the understanding we find in Diogenes by looking at another source, Sextus Empiricus, whose works are by far the most detailed and comprehensive Pyrrhonian writing surviving from antiquity. If Diogenes' *Life* of Pyrrho gives us a first approximation of Pyrrhonism, the texts of Sextus allow us to go wider and deeper.

Sextus Empiricus, writing, like Diogenes, half a millennium or so after Pyrrho, strikes an entirely different tone. He takes Pyrrho for granted as the movement's founder, and offers few details about him. Sextus presents instead an in-depth expository review of Pyrrhonism as a mature movement, a body of knowledge which, after coalescing in the person of Pyrrho, took on a life of its own in the context of Greek philosophical debate. Unlike the other major ancient schools—the Platonists, Aristotelians, Stoics, and Epicureans—Pyrrhonism was never institutionalized. Those schools all established well-known centers associated with some physical location—the Academy, the Lyceum, the Stoa, and the Garden. Pyrrhonism by contrast seems to have been passed on much more informally and without a geographical anchor, but perhaps no less effectively, by self-perpetuating social networking, as we might say today.[2] In this it may well reflect the spirit of personal philosophical practice evident, by all accounts, in Pyrrho himself, as well in early Buddhism.

We don't know the setting in which Sextus's works were written, but his texts have the flavor of lecture or monologue notes, of systematic exposition, with an occasional aside or a bit of dry wit. They cover a wide range of Pyrrhonian topics for the edification, presumably, of an audience of disciples, students, and other inquirers. His books read like a course—call it Pyrrhonism 101—delivered with the quiet assurance, objective voice, and breadth of knowledge of a true expert. We know little of Sextus except that he was a physician, and in his exhaustive survey of all possible aspects and applications of his subject we can perhaps see a systematic clinical mind at work.

Sextus' writings contain three major works of his, in whole or in part. His most influential work, leading off the Loeb series, is the complete *Outlines of Pyrrhonism*, in which Pyrrhonian understanding and practices are described in some detail, followed by in-depth Pyrrhonian assessments of the major schools of ancient Greek philosophy. The second major work is *Sceptical Treatises*, to give it its original title, which is the remaining last half of what was originally a larger work. What survives of it are three books that apply a Pyrrhonian critique to logic, physics, and ethics, respectively, as propounded by the dogmatic philosophers. Sextus' last work, also complete, *Against the Learned* (or *Professors*), reviews the claims of specialized experts as understood by the Pyrrhonists. (The last two works, though now distinguished by scholars, have previously been mixed together and mis-titled in various editions.[3]) Sextus' works are a goldmine of information not otherwise found on nearly all of the major philosophical schools of classical Western antiquity.

Sextus was one of Diogenes' sources, and all of Diogenes' summary points of Pyrrhonism—acceptance of appearances, suspension of judgment over beliefs, and tranquility (*ataraxia*)—are confirmed in Sextus. But Sextus, unlike Diogenes, writes with the authority of a Pyrrhonian practitioner. To distinguish those practices, Sextus, on the very first page of his *Outlines*, divides all philosophical investigators into three groups: first, Dogmatists such as Aristotelians, Epicureans, and Stoics who "think that they have discovered the truth," second those, including the schools of Clitomachus, Carneades, and other Academics, who "have asserted that things cannot be apprehended," and third, the Sceptics [Pyrrhonists], who "are still investigating."[4]

Although Sextus is clear that Pyrrhonism is distinct from Academic scepticism, modern commentators have found it hard to pinpoint the difference, or more precisely, the significance of the difference. They generally lump Pyrrhonists and Academics together as members of a common sceptical tradition, ignoring the objections of the Pyrrhonists.[5] To add to the confusion, Academics did not call themselves sceptics, though Pyrrhonists did—albeit using the root sense of the term as inquiry, rather than doubt. In modern times, as we've seen, scepticism has come to mean doubt about anything—about any assertion or judgment, not just those about beliefs—and it is in that sense the term applies to the Academics, not the Pyrrhonists.

What today we call pure or total scepticism—the denial that any knowledge of the nature of things is possible—is identified by Sextus with the philosophers of the middle period of Plato's Academy, beginning in the third century BCE, led by Arcesilaus, Carneades, and Clitomachus. Like the Pyrrhonists, the Academics used opposing judgments to nullify claims to knowledge. But, unlike the Pyrrhonists, who accepted appearances but not beliefs about appearances, Academics discounted appearances. They continued to presuppose that appearances must be grounded in some belief. And, being unable to establish any such belief, they dismissed appearances as unreliable illusions.

Academics (Middle Academy sceptics) share the opposition of competing judgments with the Pyrrhonists; but they do not share the tranquility said to follow. We find a clue to this when comparing Diogenes' biographies of Carneades and Pyrrho. Unlike the imperturbable yogi, Pyrrho, Carneades exhibited a kind of manic instability, exemplified in his obsession with counter-arguments and his reported desperation in the face of death. He is most famous for debating for and against virtue on successive days in Rome in 155 BCE, prompting the anger of Cato the Elder, and leading to a (temporary) banishment of philosophers from the city for a perceived display of nihilism, not liberation. Carneades, it seems, was no realized being.

Carneades was convinced, it appears, like other sceptical Academics, that no knowledge at all is possible because a counter-argument can always be found to oppose any claim to knowledge. This is to universalize doubt, to turn it into a dogma; it is to make a judgment (that such an argument can always be found) which draws a conclusion (that knowledge is impossible). This reflects the spirit of the man Academics point to as their founder: Socrates, not Pyrrho. The Pyrrhonists, by contrast, took the step Socrates never took and suspended judgment about the inevitability of counter-arguments. Unlike Socrates, they didn't claim to know that they didn't know. No wonder that Sextus and Diogenes both saw Academics as dogmatists, albeit dogmatists holding a negative rather than positive belief, but a belief just the same.

Sextus makes it plain that Pyrrhonists are sceptics, though not in the Academic (or modern) sense of those who deny that knowledge is possible. He tells us instead that "the Sceptics are still investigating,"[6] that is, they are investigating whether or not we can establish how things really are. But, Sextus cautions, "we are not to investigate how what appears appears or how what is thought of is thought of, but simply to take them for granted."[7] Both what appears (*phainomena*) and what is thought (*nooumena*), are to be accepted at face-value, or as self-evident, Sextus tells us, just as Diogenes does.

In Sextus as well as Diogenes, the "phenomena" are the objects we find in sensation, and the "noumena" are those we find in thought. I will call the latter mental phenomena, for convenience, and so use the word phenomena to include both self-evident thoughts, or "noumena," as well as self-evident sensations. We commonly speak of perceiving sensations and thoughts, but we should not assume that there is a non-evident process of perception by which objects are perceived, any more than there is one by which they are signified. Sextus (like the Buddhists) makes no such assumption, but simply points out that sensations and thoughts are our immediate, primary experiences. He neither invokes nor presupposes any prior or underlying process, but notes that phenomena simply appear, and that's what perception is. Immediate, self-evident thoughts and sensations (the mental image I contemplate, the visual form I see, the sound I hear, and so on) are the primitive elements of our experience. They themselves are not to be explained; rather they serve as the basis for any possible explanation.

Sextus points out, as we've noted, that Pyrrhonian sceptics "assent to feelings forced upon them by appearances."[8] He adds: "... the standard of the Sceptical persuasion is what is apparent, implicitly meaning by this the appearances; for they depend on passive and unwilled feelings, and are not objects of investigation."[9] Appearances for Sextus are the involuntary and undeniable phenomena we directly experience. We cannot help but have them when we have them. No one is confused about appearances as such. We know when we are hot, or cold, or have a bitter taste, or see light, or darkness, or hear a sound, or imagine something, and so forth.

This insistence on the satisfying clarity of the phenomena we actually experience is a remarkable and distinguishing feature of Pyrrhonism. None of the other major schools of ancient or modern philosophy in the West insist on this as they do. Appearances, or phenomenal sensations and thoughts, from the pre-Socratics to the post-modernists, are almost universally distrusted as irrational particulars, as fleeting, unreliable, and illusory. This is a conclusion, however, as Sextus points out, that can only be drawn if appearances are *not* taken at face value, but rather interpreted in one way or another, as, for example, when they are presumed to be a function of some non-apparent reality, of what things are imagined to be in themselves, not as we experience them.

Sextus notes that the presumption of "what things really are in themselves" is equivalent to a judgment about the external world which Pyrrhonists cannot affirm: "... they [Pyrrhonian sceptics] say what is apparent to themselves and report their own feelings without holding opinions, affirming nothing about the external objects."[10] In his discussion in the *Outlines* of the various modes for suspending judgment Sextus repeatedly makes the point that it is necessary to suspend judgment about external existing objects. In comparing Pyrrhonism with the Cyrenaic philosophy, for instance, Sextus makes the blanket statement that "we suspend judgment (as far as the argument goes) about external existing things."[11]

This is not a denial any more that it is an affirmation of the existence of the external world, but it renders the question a moot one, at least as far as our experience is concerned. It is tempting to conclude that Pyrrhonian sceptics, like Buddhists, recognize only a subjective world of sensations and thoughts. But this would be a mistake insofar as a suspension of objectivity implies a suspension of subjectivity. You can't have subjectivity without objectivity, or vice-versa. Extreme subjectivity—for example, solipsism—still presupposes objectivity, even if it's not evident or accessible.

No one doubts that they *feel* warm when they *feel* warm, or *feel* cold when they *feel* cold. There is no doubt about *what* appearances are being suffered as we suffer them, of *what* warm and cold are, for instance, or any other appearances we suffer. Our unmistakable phenomena, our sensations and thoughts, are universals in this understanding, not particulars, albeit ones which come and go and come again, and variously combine together as facts, or *pragmata*. The sights I see, the sounds I hear, and so on, including the thoughts I think, commonly recur in our experience, as far as we can tell, though often in different contexts, or combinations.

Without this reliability of recurring sensations, our world would be chaos, which it is not. Most of the time people report that they share the same sensations under the same circumstances (you and I both notice we are warm, or cold, etc.), but sometimes they do not. Either way, however, whether the sensations we experience under similar circumstances are the same or different, they remain recurring sensations that we actually do experience, directly and involuntarily. They make up for us the flow of experience, or consciousness, in which we live through the instrumentality of the body.

As far as thoughts go, Sextus takes them to be as evident as sensations. "... [A] Sceptic is not, I think, barred from having thoughts, if they arise from things which give him a passive impression and appear evidently to him and do not at all imply the reality of what is being thought of—for we can think, as they say, not only of real things but also of unreal things."[12] Sensations and thoughts, then, both have a distinct, evident, irreducible integrity. If I meet a friend in sensation (in 'reality,' or physically), he or she is presented to me involuntarily—I can't help having the sensation of my friend if I meet him or her at home, at work, or in the street. If I 'meet' my friend in thought (that is, if I imagine my friend), he or she is also represented to me involuntarily—I can't help having the thought of my friend if I think of (imagine) my friend.

My thoughts, Sextus makes clear, allow me to represent to myself (to imagine in my mind) things that are now absent but have been present to me as sensations—my memories. I can represent to myself a friend with whom I had lunch yesterday, or what my late mother looked like. Our ability to do so is extensive, detailed, and often seemingly effortless. We take our imagination for granted, although it seems a uniquely human ability, at least in scope and power; it appears far more extensive, as far as we can tell, than what's found in any other animal. Furthermore, I can also represent to myself fictional things I have *not* experienced in sensation—say, Zeus or mermaids or centaurs or Santa Claus. I might have seen pictures or models of these things in sensation, derived from someone's thought, but so far neither I (nor anyone else) has ever established seeing an actual mermaid, or centaur, or Santa Claus himself, existing independently of images imagined, or the representations of such images.

Sextus clarifies this imaginative process in a passage in "Against the Geometers," part of his book, *Against the Learned*:

> In general, also, everything conceived [*noumenon*] is conceived of in two main ways, either by way of clear impression or by way of transference from things clear, and this way is three-fold,—by similarity, or by composition, or by analogy. Thus, by clear impression are conceived the white, the black, the sweet and the

bitter, and by transference from things clear are concepts due to similarity,—such as Socrates himself from a likeness of Socrates, and those due to composition,—such as the hippocentaur from horse and man, for by mixing the limbs of horse and man we have imagined the hippocentaur which is neither man nor horse but a compound of both. And a thing is conceived by way of analogy also in two ways, sometimes by way of increase, sometimes by decrease; for instance, from ordinary men ... we conceive by way of increase the Cyclops ... and by way of decrease we conceive the pygmy whom we have not perceived through sense impressions.[13]

These possibilities—similarity, composition, and analogy—exhaust the Pyrrhonian options for mental activity. But however thoughts may be transferred, compared, or combined, both they as well as sensations retain a distinct, evident, irreducible integrity, Sextus insists. Both are equally present to us as phenomena which appear involuntarily. They cannot be distinguished as either inside or outside of us, but only as *immediately present to consciousness.* The notion that thoughts are subjective, or somehow "inside" us, or that sensations are objective, or somehow "outside" us, or that they represent things outside of us—these are all interpretations of our phenomenal experience, just the kind of judgment the Pyrrhonists tell us we should avoid.

Pyrrhonists observe that our immediate, evident objects of experience, our thoughts and sensations, are phenomena continuously in flux, and that, apparently without exception, they variously combine and recombine with one another into facts—what Sextus, like Diogenes, calls *pragmata*. Phenomena mean different things, depending on the context—the facts or *pragmata*—in which they appear: "... each thing," Sextus tells us, "appears relative to a given admixture and a given composition and quantity and position ...." And, "... since everything is relative," he says, "we shall suspend judgment as to what things are independently and in their nature."[14] So, the significance of appearances—of what they mean to us—depends wholly on the shifting factual contexts or *pragmata* in which they appear and disappear, along with other appearances. So nothing in itself, they say, is "any more this than that."

Sextus insists that we cannot deny the immediate objects of our experience, our thoughts and sensations; these are the appearances we actually experience, grouped as they are into *pragmata* or facts. Nor can we be in error about what they are. In his *Outlines of Scepticism*, Sextus writes: "Those who say that the sceptics [Pyrrhonists] reject what is apparent have not, I think, listened to what we say .... When we investigate whether existing things are such as they appear, we grant that they appear, and what we investigate is not what is apparent, but what is said about what is apparent—and this is different from investigating what is apparent itself. For example, it appears to us that honey sweetens ... but whether ... it is actually sweet is something we investigate—and this is not what is apparent but something said about what is apparent."[15]

Sextus points out that we involuntarily accept our appearances, which we experience as variously combined together into *pragmata*, or facts. Think of it this way: If it's a sunny day and I go outside, and if my eyesight is normal and I look up, I cannot help but see the sunny blue sky. Or this: If my hearing is normal and I stand next to a regular tuned-up piano, I cannot help but hear middle C if a certain key is struck. And so on for the gardenia I smell, or the fur that I touch. And similarly, if someone says "Think of your mother," I cannot help but think of my mother; or if they say "Think of the *Mona Lisa*," I cannot help but think of, that is, imagine or recollect, the *Mona Lisa*, that is, produce some mental image I have of the *Mona Lisa*.

Appearances are evident, or apparent, because they are as involuntary as they are direct and immediate. They literally force themselves upon us. We have no choice, Pyrrhonists say, but to suffer and endure them. We cannot help having them when we have them. And we invariably experience them, it seems, as facts, or *pragmata*, as complexes of phenomena. I don't just see the blue sky, I see a visual complex of sky at a certain time and place; I don't just hear Middle C, I hear a certain note struck on a certain piano in a certain room, and so on.

What is not apparent, by contrast, is what we can say *about* these experiences, or facts, that is, *how* we interpret them. To interpret an experience is to imagine something about it; it is to take it as a sign of another experience, one which is not at the moment present. On a hike in the desert, I might see a shimmering blur up ahead of me. When I do, there is no mistaking the immediate visual experience of the shimmering blur I see. It is only when I interpret the blur, when I take it for something else, say a body of water, that I can make a mistake. Appearances for the Pyrrhonists cannot in themselves be in error; error arises only when we interpret our appearances. For interpretation takes us from something evident to something non-evident, to something we could be wrong about.

This doesn't mean that our interpretations are necessarily wrong; there might in fact be water ahead in the desert. But interpretation necessarily involves some degree of uncertainty. For Sextus, like Diogenes, signs are dependently, not independently, existing. And insofar as they are dependently existing, they are phenomenally self-evident. A dependent sign is simply a phenomenon which can be correlated with another phenomenon. Sextus gives the stock examples of smoke as a sign of fire, and a scar as a sign of a wound, though even these might, in some peculiar circumstances, turn out to be wrong. But, for Pyrrhonists, it's never the appearance itself that's wrong, only our interpretation of it.

It is in his discussion of what is apparent and what is said about the apparent—of signs and signification—that Sextus comes closest to describing what we might call the phenomenalistic ontology of Pyrrhonism. If we understand ontology as the science of being—of what exists and what doesn't exist—it seems clear that Pyrrhonists too have such a science. This is a descriptive not a speculative science. Pyrrhonists claim to propound not an interpretation (opinion, belief, or theory about what supposedly does or does not exist), as they say the dogmatists do; instead what they insist they are doing is providing a self-evident, scientific account, or observation, or report, of the most basic constituents of our experience: our phenomenally composed *pragmata*. These constituents, as we've seen, are involuntary in nature; and they are taken "for granted" in ordinary experience.

Sextus discusses signs in detail in two places—in the *Outlines* and in *Against the Logicians*—using different and somewhat confusing terminology.[16] In the *Outlines*, Sextus offers a four-fold description of *pragmata* and what they can signify, or not signify:

> Some objects, then, according to the Dogmatists, are clear and some are unclear. And of the unclear, some are unclear once and for all, some are unclear for the moment, some are unclear by nature. What comes of itself to our knowledge, they say, is clear (e.g., that it is day); what does not have a nature such as to fall under our apprehension is unclear once and for all (e.g., that the stars are even in number); what has an evident nature but is made unclear for us for the moment by certain external circumstances is unclear for the moment (e.g., for me now, the city of the Athenians); and what does not have a nature such as to fall under our evident grasp is unclear by nature (e.g., imperceptible pores—for these are never apparent of themselves but would be deemed to be apprehended, if at all, by way of something else, e.g., by sweating ...).[17]

In *Against the Logicians*, Sextus makes the same distinctions using somewhat different terms. He calls *pragmata* evident or non-evident, rather than clear or unclear, and adds that they are evident as sensations and thoughts: "... of the objects apprehended by man," he writes, "some appear to be apprehended by means of sense, others by the intellect—by means of sense, as white, black, sweet, bitter; and by intellect, fair foul, lawful, lawless, pious, impious."[18] In the *Outlines* he tells us things are unclear in three ways: "for the moment," "by nature," and "once and for all." In *Logicians*, he tells us things are non-evident in three ways: "temporarily," "absolutely," and "naturally."

His examples clarify what is meant. Things absent temporarily "or for the moment" include the city of Athens (when, say, in Rome), a past wound suggested by a present scar, and the visible smoke of a hidden fire. Those things are absent at the moment, but have been or can be present. They are signified in their absence by signs which Sextus calls "recollective" in one version and "commemorative" in the others. Things absolutely or "by nature" unclear or absent include the even or odd number of stars or grains of sand in Libya. These are things by nature we see we cannot apprehend. And, most importantly, he describes things unclear "once and for all" in the *Outlines* as "naturally" non-evident in *Logicians*. These are absences "everlastingly hidden away," including notions such as the Void, or the human Soul.

The soul or self is not included among our thoughts or sensations, as Buddhists have long noted, and David Hume famously pointed out, nor do we expect the Void, or God, or Nature, or any such proposed entity, to appear among the things we perceive. None of these things are anywhere realized in our immediate sensible experience, yet they remain absences of which we are somehow aware. They are, we might say, things evidently non-evident.

I notice what is non-evident. I notice, for instance, the absence of a student who fails to come to class. The absent student is temporarily non-evident, since he or she could re-appear. The absence of an even or odd number for the stars is also evident. But because I can see both how to start counting the stars, as well as how it is that I can't finish the job, this kind of absence cannot be sensibly resolved. But the Soul and other inherently non-evident things, according to Sextus, defy any kind of sensible appearance. My Soul consistently fails to appear to me, as both the Buddhists and Hume report; it has not been and is not now present to me as are my thoughts and sensations. The Soul and other evidently non-evident things Sextus calls naturally non-evident.

We have no need of signs for appearances present to us—here Sextus agrees with the dogmatists and common practice—since we already possess these appearances. He also agrees that some phenomena are useful as signs for things temporarily non-evident, invoking the stock examples of smoke as a sign of fire, and a scar as the sign of a wound. Such signs, he says, are normally accepted and indispensable to ordinary life. And he also agrees with the dogmatists and others that signs for things "by nature" unclear or non-evident are pointless and useless because we can see that existing procedures for identifying such things cannot be applied.

So far so good. Sextus opposes, however, the idea, advanced by dogmatists, that appearances can signify things naturally or "once and for all" non-evident, such as the soul, God, truth, love, justice, knowledge, and many others. It is "the Dogmatists," Sextus charges, "who have risen up against the common judgment and declare that they discern by means of signs things naturally ['once and for all'] non-evident."[19] These are the dogmatists' so-called indicative signs. The indicative sign, Sextus tells us: "... does not ... admit of being observed in conjunction with the thing signified ... but entirely of its own nature and constitution, all but uttering its voice aloud, it is said to signify that whereof it is indicative. The soul, for instance, is one of the things naturally non-evident; for such is its nature that it never presents itself to our clear perception; and being such, it is announced 'indicatively' by the bodily motions; for we [the dogmatists, who Sextus appears to be directly quoting here] argue that it is in a certain power residing within the body which inwardly excites in it such motions."[20]

Because there is nothing stopping us from imagining what we please about things naturally non-evident, we are left free to dogmatize about them, to assert their independent existence, and to entertain the notion that we can use indicative signs to invoke what we imagine. One way to understand Sextus is to recognize that he offers a procedure, or practice—a scientific method of inquiry—for emptying indicative signs of any value, so as to be able to set them aside. He sums it up this way: "... we refute by means of natural science the Dogmatists who have risen up against the common judgment and declared that they discern by means of signs things naturally non-evident."[21]

Sextus should be understood as a scientist. He was a physician from the Methodic school, whose medical practice focused on recognizing and responding to the symptoms of the patient. Methodists rejected the competing views of the Dogmatic and Empiric schools of medicine.[22] The former sought, as one might anticipate, for an underlying, hidden cause of disease, from which they could derive a cure. The latter looked to the history and background of the patient, from which they drew their treatments. The purported hidden essence of disease sought by the Dogmatists, as well as the abstract narratives developed by the Empiricists, were both fictions, according to Sextus, which ignored the real evidence at hand: the actual symptoms.

Evidence is what is apparent, which Sextus clarifies by approvingly quoting the earlier Pyrrhonian philosopher, Aenesidemus, as follows: "For Aenesidenmus says there is a difference in things apparent, and asserts that some of them appear to all men in common, others to one person separately, and of these such as appear to all in common are true, and the other sort false."[23] Those which appear to us in common we can verify publicly; those are our sensations. Those which appear separately, or privately, we cannot verify publicly; those are our thoughts, or imaginings. Both are apparent to us, but only sensations enjoy the truth of confirmation which comes from being shared. Thoughts can be true, or realized, only if correlated with sensations; otherwise they remain evident merely as private thoughts which lack correlation with anything sensible.

Sextus, in sum, presents Pyrrhonism as a phenomenally-based science, like Methodism, in which appearances (and their absence) are the only criterion. Thoughts either accurately reflect sensations—for instance as signs of things temporarily non-evident—or they do not. Pyrrhonists insist, according to Sextus, that signs are phenomena correlated with other phenomena. If no correlation can be found, the claim to signify remains unconfirmed; it is suspended, but not falsified.

Sextus constantly returns to appearances. In a key passage from *Against the Logicians* he further clarifies what he means by appearances, or phenomena:

> Of existing things ... some ... have an absolute, others a relative, existence. Absolutely existing are all such things as are perceived with a subsistence of their own and absolutely, as for instance white, black, sweet, bitter, and everything of a similar kind for we apprehended these by themselves alone and separately and without the accompaniment of any other precept. But those things are relative which are perceived as standing in some relation to another thing and no longer apprehended absolutely (that is, separately by themselves); as, for example, the whiter and blacker and sweeter and bitterer ... For the whiter or blacker is not perceived separately in the same

way as the white or black; but in order to perceive the former, one must also apprehend along with it the object than which it is whiter, or than which it is blacker.[24]

Here we see Pyrrho's Democritean mind-set at work. Appearances are atoms, at once unambiguous in their immediate, individual manifestations, and at the same time ambiguous in their possible relations to one another. They are unambiguous as "absolutely existing," recurring elements, or atoms, and at the same time ambiguous in the facts or *pragmata* those atoms constitute. In its individual manifestation, an appearance is simply what it is; we recognize individual appearances in any context: a color, a tone, a smell, a texture, a thought, etc. But in its relations to other appearances—as part of an ensemble of appearances—any phenomenal element will contribute now to one effect in one ensemble, and then to another effect in another, and so forth, depending in each case entirely on the other appearances with which it happens to be related.

The "commemorative" signs invoked by Sextus in *Logicians* (equivalent to the "recollective" signs of the *Outlines*) indicate *pragmata* which are temporarily non-evident. The correlations between smoke and fire, or a scar and a wound, or day and night, or any number of others, are commonly and reliably established. Indeed, the discovery of such correlations is the major business of scientific inquiry. Even further, according to Sextus, similar correlations can be established by human conventions, such as laws, customs, and social practices. Different communities can establish different signifying correlations, but all that matters is that they consistently follow those they have chosen.

Sextus gives some colorful examples of social signification, common enough in his day, if not in ours: "... the raising high of a torch signifies to some the approach of enemies, but to others indicates the arrival of friends; and the sound of a bell is to some a sign of the selling of meat, but to others of the need for watering the roads."[25] He also speaks of the arrangements of sounds understood by those who know a language, but not for those who don't. Sextus is concerned to refute the flexible social use of commemorative signs by dogmatists as a justification for indicative signs:

> ... in reply to those who draw inferences from the commemorative sign and quote the case of the torch, and also of the sound of the bell, we must declare that it is not paradoxical for such signs to be capable of announcing more than one. For they are determined, as

they say, by the lawgivers and lie in our power, whether we wish them to indicate one thing or to be capable of announcing several things. But as the indicative sign is supposed to be essentially suggestive of the thing signified, it must necessarily be indicative of one thing and this must certainly be a thing of single form, since of course, if it is common to many things, it will not be a sign. For it is impossible for one object to be firmly apprehended by means of anything when the things indicated thereby are many.[26]

The indicative sign is "essentially suggestive" since it alone is said to provide the information we can get of otherwise naturally non-evident things. Yet, lacking an evident referent, an indicative sign can indicate many things, or indeed anything at all, which is to say, nothing. Sextus goes on to illustrate the point:

For example, a man's fall from wealth to poverty is a sign alike of a life of dissipation, and of disaster by sea, and of contributions to friends; and being thus common to many things, it can no longer be indicative of any one of them in special.... Nor, indeed, can it be indicative of all; for they are not all capable of co-existing.[27]

Over and over again, Sextus drives home the conclusion that judgments relying on indicative signs to determine naturally non-evident things—or beliefs—are open to an indefinite number of conflicting interpretations, and should therefore be suspended. The various Pyrrhonian modes catalogue just such different types of opposing judgments, and together illustrate the impossible task of asserting signs for non-evident referents which remain undetermined. Indicative signs are the mechanism of belief, not knowledge. As Sextus says in the *Outlines*, "if you hold beliefs, then you posit as real the things you are said to hold beliefs about."[28]

Suspension of judgment, as made clear by Sextus as well as Diogenes, is suspension of belief, the abandonment of a commitment to one or another fictional reality. The Pyrrhonists pursued the abandonment of all beliefs—of any clinging to any independent existence on the part of objects we merely imagine. They claimed to find, as a consequence, a liberation into tranquility, or *ataraxia*. The dissolution of fictional belief is simultaneously a reaffirmation of actual involuntary experience which cannot be denied. It is also an affirmation of what remains indeterminate, or naturally absent, or non-evident. Indeterminate things do not appear. They cannot be found in sensation or thought, and their existence can no more be denied than it can be affirmed. Tranquility, in this light, arises out of the recognition of indeterminacy in place of belief, the recognition of a non-specific sense of self—or of consciousness, or soul, as the Pyrrhonists would say—distinguished from the phenomenal facts of life, from our *pragmata*. The result of suspending beliefs and living with direct experience, Pyrrhonists claimed, is peace of mind, tranquility, or *ataraxia*. This is a soteriological and not merely an intellectual issue. It's not only about understanding "how things really are," though it is that too; it is about realizing a fundamental change in experience itself, a liberation from suffering from belief, which follows from understanding "how things really are." "Suspension of judgment," Diogenes reports, "... brings with it tranquility, like its shadow."[29]

Meditative or contemplative states are closely associated with this state of mind. Pyrrho, Diogenes tells us, would periodically "withdraw from the world and live in solitude."[30] The Buddha's meditative states are similarly well attested. Other ancient philosophers exhibited similar behavior. In Plato's *Symposium,* Socrates is described as falling into a sustained trace. The meditative posture he apparently practiced is perhaps what allowed him to listen to his *daemon*, as he put it, which seems to have been an ability to recognize what became apparent to him out of the uninterrupted flow of his experience. This was perhaps made possible by his own well-known suspensions of judgment. His ability to follow his *daemon*, he claimed, is what allowed him to act correctly, with moral spontaneity. The same might be said of Pyrrho and the Buddha.

The pursuit of *ataraxia*, or something like it, was widely held as a common goal of Hellenistic philosophies—not only Pyrrhonism, but Stoicism and Epicureanism as well. Pyrrhonists, however, disputed that the kind of dogmatic judgments made by Stoics and Epicureans could lead to *ataraxia* as they understood it, and Sextus is very clear, even emphatic, on distinguishing Pyrrhonism from both Stoicism and Epicureanism, as well as from all other schools. Dogmatic judgments, or beliefs, found in all the other schools are articles of faith rather than knowledge, Pyrrhonists maintain, and thereby inherently unstable. Anyone can easily reject any dogmatic claim, and substitute another in its place. In the absence of a public standard of evidence, a dogma can be maintained only by willful assertion on the part of the dogmatist. Dogmatists are thereby drawn into disputations with their critics which, by their very nature, resist resolution. Even worse, the dogmatist, confronted with criticism, is left with a simple choice: either to abandon the dogma he or she holds in favor of another dogma, or to double-down on the first dogma. Neither option is conducive to *ataraxia*.

50 Sextus Empiricus

The Epicureans believed *ataraxia* to be the absence of pain, while the Stoics believed it was the absence of passion. Unlike Epicureans and Stoics, the Pyrrhonists suspended beliefs about pleasures and pains, as well as passions. To hold such beliefs, they pointed out, is not only to assert a fictitious reality as real—it is to identify oneself with it. Identification with a belief is the result of the willful assertion necessary to maintain the belief. The Pyrrhonists, by contrast, make no such identifications. For them, the tranquility of *ataraxia* comes from the liberation of the self from such identities, from the recognition that the self is not to be found in any of the beliefs people have about themselves or their experience. We do not know who, or what, if anything, we are. The suspension of belief in an independently existing self is the suspension of belief in an imagined self, a false-self; it is the end of clinging to such a self, to any assertion of its independent existence. When and if all beliefs about all independently existing things are suspended, only the display of *pragmata* to consciousness remains— the endless river of conscious experience into which our suspended beliefs and false-selves finally dissolve. The only self that remains is the wholly indeterminate self, the self that is not present in any of the objects of consciousness, the self which neither is, nor is not, as Pyrrhonists and Buddhists alike would say.

Notes

1 I use *nirvana* rather than *nirvāṇa.* throughout, as this Sanskrit term has become normalized as an English word.
2 Pyrrho is mentioned as late as 362/3 BCE by the Emperor Julian in his "Letter to a Priest"; along with Epicurus, but notes that "the gods in their wisdom have already destroyed their works, so most of their books [*logos*] have ceased to be"; see *The Works of the Emperor Julian*, vol. 2, trans. Wilmer C. Wright (Cambridge, MA: Harvard University Press, Loeb Classical Library, 1913) 327.
3 In the Loeb classical library, *Outlines of Pyrrhonism* forms volume one; what we have of *Sceptical Treatises* (under the titles *Against the Logicians*, *Against the Physicists*, and *Against the Ethicists*) forms volumes two and three; and *Against the Learned* (under the title *Against the Professors*) forms volume four.
4 Sextus Empiricus, *Outlines of Scepticism*, trans. J. Annas and J. Barnes (Cambridge: Cambridge University Press, 1994) 3.
5 See, for example, Harald Thorsrud, *Ancient Scepticism* (Berkeley: University of California Press, 2009) *et. passim.*
6 Ibid., 3.
7 Ibid., 5.
8 Ibid., 6.
9 Ibid., 9.

10 Ibid., 7.
11 Ibid., 55.
12 Ibid., 69.
13 Sextus Empiricus, "Against the Geometers" in *Against the Professors*, trans. R. G. Bury (Cambridge, MA: Harvard University Press, Loeb Classical Library, 2000 [1949]), III, 4–43, 263–5.
14 Empiricus, *Outlines of Scepticism*, op. cit., 35.
15 Ibid., I, 19, 8.
16 See ibid., II, 97–1332, pp. 92–101, and *Against the Logicians*, trans. R. G. Bury (Cambridge, MA: Harvard University Press, 1935), II, 145–55, 315–9.
17 Ibid., II, 97, 92.
18 Ibid., II, 176, 329.
19 Ibid., 319.
20 Ibid., 317.
21 Ibid., 319.
22 Cf. "Galen" in the *Stanford Encyclopedia of Philosophy*, 18 March 2016, https://plato.stanford.edu/entries/galen/.
23 Empiricus, *Against the Logicians* op. cit., II, 8, 243.
24 Ibid., 321–3.
25 Ibid., 339.
26 Ibid., 343.
27 Ibid., 343.
28 Empiricus, *Outlines of Scepticism*, op. cit., 6.
29 Laertius, op. cit., II, 517–18.
30 Ibid., 477.

4 Timon and Aulus Gellius

The third major source for Pyrrhonism, after Diogenes Laertius and Sextus Empiricus, is Timon of Phlius, the most prominent and influential of Pyrrho's immediate disciples. Between his interesting lives of Pyrrho and Epicurus, Diogenes sandwiched a tantalizingly brief sketch of Timon. Like his master, Pyrrho, Timon was a colorful character. Orphaned at an early age, Diogenes tells us, he became a stage-dancer, perhaps against his will. He left the theater, disliking dancing, and found his way to his first teacher, the Megaric philosopher Stilpo. Pyrrho is said by Diogenes to have studied with Bryson, an obscure philosopher connected with Stilpo. Stilpo and Bryson were both associated with the Megarian school of philosophy, derived from Socrates, which focused on logical argumentation among two or more interlocutors—what came to be known as dialectics. Megarian philosophers, including one Menedemus, were active in Elis, and it may have been through the Megarians that Timon heard of Pyrrho and perhaps got it in his mind to study with him; when he eventually did so he brought along his wife, Diogenes adds, and their children were born there.

A fragment of Timon's *Pytho*, preserved by Aristocles, a peripatetic philosopher of the first century CE, tells a somewhat different story. It has Timon, still in his stage career, on his way to perform at Delphi, when he encounters by a shrine on the road a man who is also apparently headed to Delphi, but seemingly without any clear purpose. This man was Pyrrho, it turned out, and the drama of his ability to live without intentions was somehow revealed to Timon in this meeting, and so affected him that he is said to have abandoned his stage career to go off and study with him. Aristocles, a dogmatist, has little sympathy for Pyrrhonian skepticism, but he leaves little doubt that Timon was struck by an encounter with a holy man, one who evidently displayed extra-human qualities of behavior, a yogi, and that he was transfixed for life as a result.

However their association was established, the apprenticeship with Pyrrho was decisive for Timon, who became not only a sceptical philosopher in the Pyrrhonian sense, but an apostle of Pyrrho, and arguably his most important successor. Later, finding himself in need of money, according to Diogenes, Timon left Pyrrho and embarked on what scholar and historian Dee L. Clayman describes as a career in "the international network of writers, artists, and intellectuals."[1] Timon and his cultivated colleagues and competitors lived as professional philosophers, or sophists, mostly on the patronage of Hellenistic monarchs, as they moved from court to court, falling in and out of favor. Timon himself was personally known, Diogenes reports, to the Hellenistic kings Antigonus Gonatas and Ptolemy Philadelphus.

Having finally made his fortune, Diogenes continues, Timon settled in Athens, where he lived most of the rest of his life. A one-eyed man (oddly, like his friend King Antigonus), he was fond of wine, Diogenes reports, and wrote prolifically, including "epics, tragedies, satyric damas, thirty comedies, and sixty tragedies, besides *silli* (lampoons) and obscene poems."[2] Like Pyrrho, perhaps, "when disturbed by maid servants and dogs, he would stop writing, his earnest desire being to attain tranquility."[3]

The anecdotes offered by Diogenes suggest that Timon developed into another yogi, just as Pyrrho had; they focus on his concentration to the point of distraction from ordinary affairs: "He used to let his own poems lie about," Diogenes says, "sometimes half-eaten away. Hence, when he came to read parts of them ... he would turn over the pages and recite whatever came handy; then, when he was half through, he would discover the piece he had been looking for in vain, so careless was he. Furthermore he was so easy-going that he would readily go without his dinner."[4]

Some fragments of Timon about Pyrrho are worth pondering: "Truly," Timon is reported as saying by Aristocles, "no other mortal could rival Pyrrho."[5] In a fragment preserved by Athenaeus of Attaleia, writing in the first century BCE, we find this, which resonates deeply with Buddhist thinking: "Timon quite splendidly said: 'Desire is absolutely the first of all bad things.'"[6] And Diogenes reports these words of Timon's about his mentor: "O old man, O Pyrrho, how and whence did you discover escape from servitude to the opinions and empty theorising of sophists? How did you unloose the shackles of every deception and persuasion?"[7]

Finally, there is this paeon by Timon, also reported by Sextus:

> This, O Pyrrho, my heart yearns to hear, how on earth you, though a man, act most easily and calmly, never taking thought

and consistently undisturbed, heedless of the whirling motions and sweet voice of wisdom? You alone lead the way for men, like the god who drives around the whole earth as he revolves, showing the blazing disk of his well-rounded sphere.[8]

As these passages suggest, Timon was an enthusiastic as well as an effective advocate for the new sceptical wisdom he found in Pyrrho. Both he and Pyrrho by all accounts rejected the Megaric school, which in fact provoked their criticism. Timon writes of "the madness of argument" the Megarics displayed.[9] He strove to develop instead the indifference he learned from Pyrrho as an antidote to the evils of competing beliefs, or dogmas, including those of the Megarians.

Clayman suggests Timon achieved this indifference through a kind of radical relativism derived from Pyrrho. She notes they both use stories as mutually canceling exemplars, and points out, as an example, the paradoxical interaction between two images drawn separately by Diogenes in his life of Pyrrho: one of a pig calmly eating on a ship in a storm with a terrified crew, and the other of Pyrrho himself taking care of pigs. The effect, she suggests, is to juxtapose the idea of a pig as a philosopher with the idea of a philosopher, if not a pig, then at least a swineherd—the point being to bring into focus the neutralizing play of opposing values so as to relieve one of competing beliefs.

The fact that appearances are relative doesn't mean that they are unreliable, as we've seen. They are exactly what they are—involuntarily experienced phenomena arranged so as to display facts (*pragmata*)—even if the facts displayed by varying combinations of appearances can lead to different, and even contradictory, conclusions. We find in Diogenes evidence that Timon, like Pyrrho, was not only a relativist about appearances, or thoughts and sensations, but also that he insisted on their primacy, as did Diogenes and Sextus: "He was constantly in the habit," Clayman notes, "of quoting, to those who would admit the evidence of the senses when confirmed by the judgment of the mind, the line—'birds of a feather flock together.'"[10] In our physical being, as animals, Timon seems to be saying, we respond naturally and in agreement with our direct experience of things, with no more needed. And, in his *Life* of Pyrrho, Diogenes quotes Timon saying in his *Images*, or *Indalmoi*: "But the apparent is omnipotent wherever it goes."[11] Timon, like Pyrrho, seems to have achieved an ability to live and work largely if not entirely within the immediate flow of experience.

Clayman, in her work on Timon, makes the interesting observation that Pyrrho was a painter, that Apelles, the famous painter, was part of Alexander's entourage, and that painterly metaphors are scattered throughout the accounts given by Diogenes, Sextus, and Timon. Sextus, in "Against the Logicians", notes that Anaxarchus, Pyrrho's early mentor, whom he accompanied in Alexander's campaigns, "likened," as did the Cynic Monimus, "existing things to a scene-painting and supposed them to resemble the impressions experienced in sleep or madness."[12] Diogenes, apparently quoting Timon, says: "When we say a picture has projections [depth], we are describing what is apparent; but if we say that it has no projections, we are then speaking, not of what is apparent, but of something else."[13] The picture, say a landscape or portrait, is not what it appears to be; it appears to be three-dimensional, but is actually only two-dimensional. None of the *pragmata* that make up our thoughts and sensations, we can conclude, can be presumed to be any of the things they seem to represent; they are rather a screen in which sensible and mental elements are variously combined, dissolved, and recombined in the panorama of consciousness.

Just what exactly do the Pyrrhonians mean by the phenomena which appear (and disappear)? Just what are the uninterpreted, involuntary thoughts and sensations that we actually experience? Just how can we separate what is interpreted from what is not interpreted? The notion of uninterpreted experience has been a hard sell in Western philosophy. If interpretation is understood, following the Pyrrhonists, as an act of non-evident belief about something evident, then what's left—the immediate empirical reality of our senses and thoughts—seems bewildering to most people. Without interpretation, many conclude, there seems to be only chaos—the "blooming, buzzing confusion" which William James presumed to be the first experience of a newborn infant.

The most systematic modern attempt to describe (not explain or interpret) the nature of phenomena is the phenomenological movement of the twentieth century, initiated by Edmund Husserl and continued by Martin Heidegger, Jean-Paul Sartre, Maurice Merleau-Ponty, and others. David Woodruff Smith offers a concise summary of the project of phenomenology as follows:

> Phenomenology is the study of structures of consciousness as experienced from the first-person point of view. The central structure of an experience is its intentionality, its being directed toward something, as it is an experience of or about some object. An experience is directed towards an object by virtue of its content or meaning (which represents the object) together with appropriate enabling conditions.[14]

There is no space nor the need to develop here a detailed comparison between modern phenomenology and ancient Pyrrhonian phenomenalism, yet the contrast between their approaches is revealing. They both share the first-person view of phenomena of which we are conscious. But the Pyrrhonists do not distinguish between the experience of an object and the object being experienced. To them, these are one and the same. To the phenomenologists, on the other hand, a distinction remains between experience and what is being experienced.

Husserl put his phenomenological understanding of appearances this way:

> Cognitive mental processes [appearances] (and this belongs to their essence) have an *intentio*, they refer to something, they are related in this or that way to an object. This activity of relating itself to an object belongs to them even if the object itself does not. And what is objective can appear, can have a certain kind of givenness in appearance, even though it is at the same time neither genuinely (*reell*) within the cognitive phenomenon, nor does it exist in any other way as a *cogitatio*. To explain the essence of cognition and the essential connections which belong to it and to bring this to self-givenness, this involves examining both these sides of the matter; it involves investigating this relatedness which belongs to the essence of cognition.[15]

Husserl's approach to phenomena makes sense only on the supposition that uninterpreted phenomena do not exist in any coherent way. For him, any uninterpreted phenomenon we experience can make sense *only* if it can "relate itself to an object"; and the business of phenomenology is to isolate such objects through a series of reductions culminating in the recovery of the "essence," which is the object itself. Such objects are the pure or elemental constituents which make up our experience, and isolating them is no easy enterprise.

It is hard to imagine a more striking contrast than this to the Pyrrhonian understanding of appearances, whose structure is displayed not upon inference or analysis or otherwise through some indirect, complex process, but is instead immediately and fully present from the start. The phenomena we experience, Pyrrhonists insist, are not chaotic or random, but highly structured, as evident in the *pragmata* they invariably combine to display. For the Pyrrhonists, our thoughts and sensations come to us providing their own content. They did not presume that our immediate experience needed to be separately structured to make sense. Sights, sounds, tastes, smells, and touches already speak, as it were, a kind of natural language, one which we can reflect in our thoughts, and which, though variable and sometimes surprising, is usually reliable, and is what leads us down the road of experience. And it is on this direct basis, not on any interpretation of it, that, Pyrrhonists hold, we should regulate our behavior.

To sum up so far: Timon confirms the testimony of Diogenes and Sextus that there are no external or internal worlds for Pyrrho, only a flowing panorama, of appearances, or thoughts and sensations, which are immediately and involuntarily evident to consciousness. This flow represents a range of representations and contrasts, presences and absences, mixed up in a stream of consciousness whose phenomenal elements come and go, with degrees of sameness and difference, embodied in a variety of *pragmata*, or facts. The trouble arises when we interpret these evident phenomena as if they were signs for non-evident things—as we saw in our discussion of Sextus.

The best evidence of this understanding of experience by Timon comes from his most famous fragment, also preserved by Aristocles, the much-debated "Aristocles passage," which has come down to us due to its inclusion in a fourth century work by the church father, Eusebius. Aristocles was a source hostile to Pyrrhonism, yet what he reports is consistent with our developing understanding of who the Pyrrhonists were.

A full translation of the Aristocles passage, by A. A. Long, is as follows:

> It is supremely necessary to investigate our own capacity for knowledge. For if we are so constituted that we know nothing, there is no need to continue inquiry into other things. Among the ancients too there have been people who made this pronouncement, and Aristotle has argued against them. Pyrrho of Elis was also a powerful spokesman of such a position. He himself has left nothing in writing, but his pupil Timon says that whoever wants to be happy must consider these three questions: first, how are things by nature. Secondly, what attitude should we adopt towards them? Thirdly, what will be the outcome for those who have this attitude? According to Timon, Pyrrho declared that things are equally indifferent, unmeasurable and inarbitrable. For this reason, neither our sensations nor our opinions tell us truths or falsehoods. Therefore for this reason we should not put our trust

in them one bit, but we should be unopinionated, uncommitted and unwavering, saying concerning each individual thing that it no more is than is not, or both is and is not, or it neither is or is not. The outcome for those who actually adopt this attitude, says Timon, will be first speechlessness, and then freedom from disturbance; and Aenesidemus says pleasure. There are the main points of what they say.[16]

The key word here translated as "things" is *pragmata*, as we might expect. We have already seen in Diogenes and Sextus that Pyrrhonism purports to tell us exactly what things (*pragmata*) are, namely, that they are evident phenomena grouped into facts, understood as a description of our actual experience, not a theory or interpretation of that experience. When Timon says that *pragmata* "are equally indifferent, unmeasurable and inarbitrable," he is saying that no *pragma*, no fact of experience, has any privileged comparison with any other, and so cannot be revealed or defined through any such comparison. No fact, in short, can be made the standard for any other fact; each fact is necessarily just what we experience, and nothing else. Differentiation, measurement, and arbitration are all comparative functions, and none of them can be said to be definitive of any fact—as the Pyrrhonian modes sought to demonstrate by putting facts into comparison (or opposition) to one another.

Thus, as Timon goes on to say, "neither our sensations nor our opinions tell us truths or falsehoods." This is to say that neither sensations nor opinions (*doxai*, or imagined dogmas, or beliefs) yield any knowledge beyond themselves; they can only display themselves, so to speak, not anything else. As a result we are to be without opinions (beliefs), and so uncommitted (to any belief), and unwavering in our refusal to endorse beliefs. So when Timon tells us that facts (*pragmata*) are "equally indistinguishable, unmeasurable and indeterminate," we can understand him to mean that no fact can be distinguished, measured, or determined more or less than any other fact, or by any other fact. They are equally distinguishable because they all appear involuntarily to consciousness; in this sense, no fact is more or less real than any other, as far as we can tell. They are equally unmeasurable (incomparable) since any fact can be judged in relation to any other fact, and so can be given virtually any meaning at all. And facts are equally indeterminate since they determine only themselves, and not anything else.

If "neither our sensations nor our opinions [*doxai*] tell us truths or falsehoods," as Timon tells us, it is because they refer only to themselves, and nothing else. To say an act of perception is true or false is to say that it says something true or false about something else; it is to make a judgment. And when Timon says "we should not put our trust in them one bit" he is in effect asking us to dispense with judgments. We should understand this to mean not that we should distrust phenomenally created facts as such, but rather that we should not trust them as *interpretations* of other facts. And when he concludes that all we can say about "each individual thing" is that it "no more is than is not, or that it both is and is not, or that it neither is nor is not," he is telling us that the existence of each individual thing, or fact, is not a matter of judgment. It is not up to us to decide *about* the involuntary facts we experience; all we can do is experience them.

The formula with which Timon concludes—that no thing (*pragma*) is more than it is not, or that it both is and is not, or that it neither is nor is not—has come down in the philosophical literature in both Greek and Buddhist traditions as the so-called quadrilemma—a choice between four options, or outcomes. It turns out, according to Pyrrhonian Buddhism as proposed in this book, that any simple judgment (X = Y) lands us in a quadrilemma. If we make the judgment that X = Y, then the following four options unavoidably present themselves: X = Y can either be 1) true, or 2) false, or 3) it can be neither true or false, or finally, 4) it can be both true and false.

The Greek term, *lemma*, at the root of quadrilemma, has the meaning of a "taking," that is, of an appropriation, or act of assertion. We can understand denial as a negative assertion. The initial choice between asserting or denying a judgment constitutes a dilemma, or two-fold choice: X = Y is either true or false. The further choice that X = Y is neither true or false, presents a third option, a suspension of judgment, which expands the dilemma into a trilemma. Finally, the last choice, that X = Y is both true and false, accepts the suspension of judgment. It presents the fourth and final option, completing the quadrilemma. If a judgment is neither true nor false, it cannot exist at all. If it is both true and false it can exist, but only as a fiction, as something imagined in thought but not realized in sensation.

Timon's summary of Pyrrhonism in terms of the four-fold logic of the quadrilemma can be simply stated:

1 Assertion (of judgment)
2 Denial (of judgment)
3 Suspension (of judgment)
4 Tranquility (freedom from judgment)

Any assertion that can be denied, or contradicted, can only be the object of what Sextus called an indicative sign, as we saw in the last chapter, not of a commemorative (or recollective) sign. The latter, as we've seen in Sextus, are signs of things temporarily non-evident, whose utility is recognized by the Pyrrhonists, while the former are said, by the dogmatists, to be the signs of things naturally non-evident, such as God, the Soul, justice, love, evil, etc.—all of which the Pyrrhonists dispute. An assertion of a commemorative sign depends on its representing something real, that its referent has at least the potential to be realized in sensation. But, insofar as anything that fails to appear in sensation cannot have its existence confirmed, we move first to a situation of dilemma, where competing assertions are made which cannot be adjudicated, and then, logically, to a recognition of trilemma, and ultimately, quadrilemma.

Fictions appear only in the mind, as thoughts, or mental images. They exist in sensation only in a secondary sense, when and if they are subsequently projected there from our thoughts (most notably in language and art). The fictions of the Pyrrhonists are the beliefs of the dogmatists, which the former suspend, but the latter presume, wrongly, to be the really existing referents of commemorative signs. The range of fiction-belief thus unleashed can hardly be overestimated. A fictional belief can be any imaginative construct from Santa's workshop to the divinity of Jesus to the dictatorship of the proletariat. A fiction becomes a belief only if and when we assert the reality of Santa Claus, or Jesus as God, or the coming dictatorship of the proletariat.

Conflicts between assertions and denials of judgment such as these—catalogued in the various modes of the Pyrrhonists and outlined by Timon—are resolved into suspension of judgment by the application of Pyrrhonian practice. Suspension in turn is the precondition for tranquility, or liberation from belief, which makes possible the ability to live, unperturbed and enlightened, in the immediate experience of the moment.

Aulus Gellius, unlike Timon, was no Pyrrhonist, but a cultured Roman grammarian of the second century CE, at the height of the empire. His *Attic Nights* is a miscellaneous collection of essays and notes on a wide variety of subjects written nearly half a millennium after Timon. In a short chapter of about two pages, entitled "Some brief notes about the Pyrrhonian Philosophers and the Academics; and of the difference between them," we find a lucid and largely overlooked summary of what Pyrrhonism meant to the educated public at the height of the Roman Empire.

Gellius, like Sextus, describes the Pyrrhonian sceptics, in contrast to the Academics, as "inquirers" and "investigators" who "decide nothing and determine nothing" but consider that "which it is possible to decide and determine."[17] Although Pyrrhonians undergo experiences just as anyone else does, such as "seeing and hearing," they remain "in doubt," Gellius tells us, not about those experiences as such, but about "the nature and character of those very things which cause them those experiences." Gellius couldn't be much clearer: for the Pyrrhonists there was a basic distinction between things which could be decided (or clarified, or understood), and those which could not.

Gellius goes on to offer an interesting summary of the Pyrrhonian understanding of what we actually experience:

> ... they say that appearances ... are produced from all objects, not according to the nature of the objects themselves, but according to the condition of mind or body of those to whom those appearances come. Therefore they call absolutely all things that affect men's senses *ta pros ti*. This expression means that there is nothing at all that is self-dependent or which has its own power or nature, but that absolutely all things have "reference to something else" and seem to be such as their appearance is while they are seen, and such as they are formed by our senses, to which they come, not by the things themselves, from which they have proceeded.[18]

The notion that "there is nothing at all that is self-dependent" is as succinct a statement of dependent origination as can be found in any Buddhist text. For Gellius, this means that our appearances are "formed by our senses ... not by the things themselves." Not being a Pyrrhonist, it is hardly surprising that he slips into non-Pyrrhonian language when he talks about appearances coming or proceeding from the things themselves, even if he recognizes that they are formed by the senses and not by the things he thinks they come from. Sextus, we remember, was quite adamant about the Pyrrhonists "... affirming nothing about external objects."[19] Gellius does transmit, however, the primacy of appearances which is so central to the Pyrrhonists, even if he doesn't think through what it fully means.

Gellius is recorded as studying with two Greek philosophers, a well-known Platonist, Lucius Calvenus Tarsus, and a more colorful character, the Cynic Peregrinus Proteus. Proteus, accused as a paricide in his youth, escaped from Syria to a Christian community in Palestine, where he was imprisoned by the Romans. Later, expelled from the Christian community, he became a Cynic, living first in Pyrrho's home town, Ellis, and eventually in Rome. In an extraordinary gesture, he announced at the Olympic Games of 161 CE that he would immolate himself at the next games, in 165, which in fact he did. A controlled self-immolation requires an almost inhuman level of self-discipline and concentration. Proteus was no exotic Indian, like Kalanos, but a local Syrian Greek, which suggests that practical techniques of self-discipline of mind and body practiced in India and appropriate to something like self-immolation were also available, and to some extent internalized, in the Greco-Roman classical world, at least for those, like Proteus, who wished to seek them out.

With Tarsus and Proteus as his poles of reference, Gellius spanned a good range of classical philosophy and practice. In his remarks on Pyrrhonism he cites only one source, the Gallic Academic philosopher Favorinus, and he strongly recommends his book, the now lost *Pyrrhonian Principles*, which Gellius says was written with "great keenness and subtlety." Gellius is pretty clearly seeing Pyrrhonism through the Academic eyes of Favorinus, but he does try, like others, to outline the difference between the two, saying that "... the Academics do, as it were, 'comprehend' the very fact that nothing can be comprehended, and, as it were, decide that nothing can be decided, while the Pyrrhonians assert that not even that can by any means be regarded as true, because nothing can be regarded as true."[20]

It has not been clear to many, then and now, just what hangs on the difference between Academics and Pyrrhonists, as we have seen, which Gellius calls "a question of long standing."[21] The impression he leaves is one of a curious philosophical quibble, but the difference between Academics and Pyrrhonists is far more profound than that. We find a clue to its importance in Gellius' interesting invocation of "the language which they say was used by Pyrrho, the founder of that philosophy: 'Does not this matter stand so, rather than so, or is it neither?'"[22] Notice that here we have the first three steps of the quadrilemma, presumably adopted from Favorinus, but not the fourth. The third step of the quadrilemma—that the disputed matter in question is neither one way or another, neither this way nor that way—draws the conclusion that neither way is the case, and more generally that nothing is the case: this is the negative dogmatic view of the Academics as described by Sextus at the very beginning of his *Outlines*.

Pyrrhonists, however, unlike Academics, do not stop at this point—that nothing in dispute can be the case, one way or the other—but go on to recognize that there is just as much a positive sense in which the disputed alternatives are both the case as well as neither being the case, that they are not nothing, but have some kind of undeniable force. This is the fourth and final step in the Pyrrhonian quadrilemma, which moves them beyond the Academics. The latter, though recognizing that any judgment about anything non-evident could be cancelled out by an opposing judgment, continued to rely on the presumption that the truth of things non-evident depends on its being revealed by *some* judgment about them. The inability to establish any such judgment led Academics to conclude that no truth about things non-evident was possible at all. Hence their negative dogmatism, or nihilism.

If truth is presumed to be a matter of judgment about things non-evident, and if nothing is evident and everything requires such a judgment, then nothing can be recognized as the experience that it is, but only as something else—it can only be an illusion. So say the Academics. But if truth is not presumed to be a matter of judgment about things non-evident, then it is possible to recognize that things simply appear as they do, as direct and involuntary thoughts and sensations. The Pyrrhonists rejected the Academic presumption that the truth of things can be revealed *only* by some judgment we can make about them, that is, that the truth of things is located somewhere other than in what appears.

The fact is, Pyrrhonists say, that I can manage with appearances only. I can connect smoke and fire, or a scar and a wound, as we saw in Sextus; these are reliable correlations which we can usually substantiate. But as long as I cannot connect one thing with another, as long as something I can imagine (a mermaid or a centaur, or love or justice) cannot be independently located in sensation, then any judgment about it (about its realization, or not, in sensation) must remain suspended. This does not mean that nothing can be known, as the Academics concluded. It only means that some judgments remain indeterminate, at least for now.

Suspension of judgment is not the end in itself that the Academics made of it; it is rather a step towards what the Pyrrhonists understood as a final conclusion: the recognition that our experience as we have it not only lacks some kind of determination from outside, but is in fact made up of wholly of appearances, and their absence, and that these appearances do not signify independently existing entities, but are mutually dependent phenomena combined into various facts or *pragmata*, some of which can be correlated pragmatically and scientifically, while others cannot. The recognition that evident appearances, instead of non-evident objects, are the coin of experience, along with the ability to distinguish those appearances which can be correlated from those which cannot, is what allowed Pyrrhonists to clarify the nature of experience, rather than distort it, and to find tranquility in the process.

Notes

1. Dee L. Clayman, *Timon of Phlius* (Berlin: Walter de Gruyter, 2009) 17.
2. Laertius, op. cit., vol. II, 521.
3. Ibid., 523.
4. Ibid., 523–5.
5. A. A. Long and D. N. Sedley, *The Hellenistic Philosophers*, vol. 1 (Cambridge: Cambridge University Press 1992) 18.
6. Ibid., 20.
7. Laertius, op. cit., vol. II, IX, 64, 479.
8. Quoted by A. A. Long and D. N. Sedley, op. cit., 19.
9. Clayman, op. cit., 8.
10. Ibid., 525.
11. Diogenes, op. cit., 517.
12. Sextus Empiricus, "Against the Logicians," I, 88, in *Against the Logicians*, trans. R. G. Bury, Loeb Classical Library, Cambridge, MA: Harvard University Press, 1997) 47.
13. Diogenes Laertius, *Lives of Eminent Philosophers*, vol. IX, 105, trans. R. D. Hicks (Cambridge: Cambridge University Press, 2000) 515.
14. David Woodruff Smith, "Phenomenology" in *Stanford Encyclopedia of Philosophy* (revised 16 December 2013) https://plato.stanford.edu/entries/phenomenology/.
15. Edmund Husserl, *The Idea of Phenomenology*, trans. Alston and Nakhnikian (The Hague: Martinus Nijhoff, 1964) 43.
16. Long and Sedley, op. cit., 14–15.
17. Aulus Gellius, *Attic Nights*, vol. II, trans. John C. Rolfe (Cambridge, MA: Harvard University Press, 1927) 309–13.
18. Ibid., 309–13.
19. Empiricus, *Outlines of Scepticism*, op. cit., I, 7, 15.
20. Gellius, *Attic Nights II*, vol. 8, book 11, op. cit., 313.
21. Ibid., 311.
22. Ibid.

5 *Pragmata* and dependent origination

The earliest texts we have for ancient Pyrrhonism and early Buddhism, apart from Timon's compressed summary preserved in the Aristocles passage, were written early in the common era, independently of one another, and centuries after the lifetimes of Pyrrho and the Buddha. Nevertheless, they display a series of remarkable parallels. Pyrrhonian talk about mutually defining appearances, evident and non-evident, present and absent, is matched by Buddhist talk about the dependent origination of impermanent phenomenal states. Pyrrhonian rejection of dogmatic belief about things inherently non-evident is matched by Buddhist rejection of clinging, or attachment, to things non-evident. Pyrrhonian suspension of judgment regarding beliefs is matched by the 'unanswered questions' of the Buddha. Pyrrhonian rejection of positive and negative dogmatisms is matched by the Buddhist rejection of eternalism and annihilationism. The open, evidence-based inquiry advanced by the Pyrrhonists is matched by the Middle Path of the Buddhists. The Pyrrhonian rejection of the interpretation of facts is matched by the Buddhist assertion of the "emptiness" of experience. And finally, the imperturbability of the Pyrrhonists, or *ataraxia*, is matched by the enlightenment or liberation of the Buddhists, or *bodhi*.

These parallels are so striking that it is impossible not to consider that both traditions derive from a singular source: a common insight into the nature of human experience first realized by the Buddha, and shared by Pyrrho. The task remaining is to reconstruct this proposed original source—the *tertium quid*—insofar as it informs the two subsequent traditions, and appears to lie at their core. The contrasts in language and idiom, custom and culture, between Greeks and Indians nonetheless reflect, in two separate mirrors, a singular account of human experience. The method for this reconstruction is R. G. Collingwood's historical imagination, in which past events are reenacted in the historian's mind. It requires merging the common elements of the two ancient traditions, and then connecting the dots where they overlap, so to bring those traditions into a single focus—as might have occurred, for instance, in sustained philosophical discussions at Alexander's court between Greeks and Indians. The picture that emerges from this synthesis we can call Pyrrhonian Buddhism.

The previous chapters have reviewed the most important sources for our understanding of Pyrrhonism; this, and succeeding, chapters will trace the common picture which emerges when Pyrrhonian and Buddhist points of contact are compared. By contrast to the relatively small body of remarkably consistent texts which have come down to us from the Pyrrhonists, even the earliest recorded Buddhist texts are voluminous, diversified, and complex. The three *Piṭakas* of the Pāli canon alone are overwhelming in their extent (running to thousands of pages), and bewildering in their apparent disorganization (with little structure, thematic or chronological, persistent ambiguity over key points, and numerous variants and repetitions). Beyond this, centuries of sometimes conflicting commentary have further complicated questions of meaning.

Nonetheless, we can recognize in the already 'normative' Buddhist tradition of the first texts the unfolding of implications inherent in early Buddhism, but perhaps not fully evident in what was initially recalled of the Buddha's sayings. To dispel the mystery of early Buddhism we are fortunate to have the aid of the Pyrrhonian texts, of which the Timon passage from Aristocles stands as the earliest known testimony we have for what we can know of early Buddhism.

Although some Buddhists texts will be cited in what follows, the range and complexity of the Buddhist tradition, unlike Pyrrhonism, is found in no single text or school, but rather in the dialectic among a variety of schools. This sprouting and unfolding of the Buddhist kernel is most famously dramatized by the imagery of the Three Turnings of the Wheel of *Dharma*—a rubric, it turns out, which closely parallels the major insights of Pyrrhonism. What the Pyrrhonists call the fluctuating, mutually defining phenomena which comprise *pragmata*, evident and non-evident, the Buddhists in the First Turning call the impermanent, dependent nature of the things we experience; both traditions share a common ontology of phenomenalistic atomism.

What the Pyrrhonists call suspension of judgment, or of the interpretation of things non-evident, the Buddhists in the Second Turning call emptiness—the final dissolution of attachments, or dogmatic beliefs (positive or negative, eternalist or annihilationist). The dogmatic beliefs suspended by Pyrrhonists are similarly put aside as 'unanswered questions' by the Buddhists, while leaving open what the Buddhist call the Middle Path of direct experience, which corresponds to the empirical science of the Pyrrhonists. And what the Pyrrhonists call *ataraxia*, the Buddhists of the Third Turning call *bodhi*, the final or perfected enlightenment. These are the parallels we shall explore in the remainder of this work.

The earliest record of the Three Turnings is found in the *Saṃdhinirmocana Sūtra* from the second century CE, in Chapter Seven, "The Questions of Paramarthasamudgata."[1] The First Turning in this text is identified with the Buddha's first sermon in the Deer Park, near Banaras, in which the "aspects of the four truths [the Four Noble Truths] of the Āryas" were taught on the nature and cessation of suffering. The Buddha, the text goes on to tell us, on another occasion, at Vulture Peak, "turned a second wheel of doctrine which is more wondrous still ... because of the aspect of teaching emptiness, beginning with the lack of own-being of phenomena, and beginning with their absence of production, absence of cessation, quiescence from the start, and being naturally in a state of nirvana."

However, the *Saṃdhinirmocana* points out, "this [second] wheel of doctrine ... is surpassable, provides an opportunity [for refutation], is of interpretable meaning, and serves as a basis of dispute." As a result, "the Bhagavān [the Buddha] turned a third wheel of doctrine, possessing good differentiations, and exceedingly wondrous...." But then the text merely repeats, by way of elaboration, the gloss from the Second Turning: "... beginning with the lack of own-being of phenomena, and beginning with their absence of production, absence of cessation, quiescence from the start, and being naturally in a state of nirvana."

The text nonetheless draws two distinctions between the Second and Third Turnings: the vastly greater scale of the Third (indicated by the enormous amount of "merit" it is said to carry), and its resistance to interpretation, and thereby disputation. Indeed, it is announced as no less than "the teaching of the ultimate, the definite meaning," which is, it seems, no less than complete enlightenment, or *bodhi*.

As far as modern scholars go, the Three Turnings have been variously linked historically, perhaps most commonly under the rubrics of *hīnayāna*, *mahāyāna*, and *vajrayāna*. Some scholars have offered more nuanced readings. Jay Garfield, for instance, writes of the First Turning as the recognition of suffering and impermanence as the path to liberation, of the Second Turning as the discovery of emptiness, and of the Third Turning as the end of dualism in Yogācāra, or the Mind-Only school.[2]

Another scholar, James Blumenthal, like Garfield, similarly sees the First Turning in the Buddha's first sermon with the Four Noble Truths, and the Second Turning in the discovery of emptiness, beginning with the Perfection of Wisdom Sūtras and culminating in the work of Nāgārjuna and the Middle Way school. With regard to the Third Turning, Blumenthal too locates its emergence in the Yogācāra, or Mind-Only school, as most fully explicated by Asaṅga and his half-brother Vasubandhu. "[T]he specific description of emptiness in the Mind-Only school," writes Blumenthal, "differs from that of the Middle Way school [of the Second Turning]. The Mind-Only school sees an object's emptiness as a lack of essence that is distinct or separate from that of the consciousness perceiving it. For the Middle Way school, phenomena are empty of their own unchanging nature. For the Mind-Only school, phenomena are empty of subject-object duality. They do not have a nature that is different from the consciousness that perceives them."[3]

A further commentator, Tenshin Reb Anderson, offers a different account of the Three Turnings: "The first turning of the wheel constructed a path of liberation, the second turning refutes the path, and the third turning accepts the refutation of the path and redeems the path. This scripture offers a path based on the refutation of the earlier path but redeems the earlier path. Another way to say it is that the first turning gives the logic of liberation, the second condemns all logic, and the third reconstructs logic but based on the understanding that logic is ultimately completely useless. In fact, the third phase used logic more than ever before, and it could use logic more energetically because it was based on the emptiness of logic."[4]

And yet another scholar, Dan Lusthaus, sums up the Turnings this way:

> The first turning, by emphasizing entities (dharmas, aggregates, etc.) while 'hiding' emptiness, might lead one to hold a substantialistic view; the second turning, by emphasizing negation while "hiding" the positive qualities of the Dharma, might be misconstrued as nihilism. The third turning was a middle way between these extremes that finally made everything explicit.[5]

Still other accounts of the Turnings could be invoked, but these are perhaps sufficient. Buddhist thought is often non-linear, as these overlapping yet distinct summaries suggest. Like Pyrrhonism,

Pragmata and dependent origination 69

Buddhism is geared to the varying capacities of its auditors, which means that there will be varying versions offered of what is presumed to be a singular description of reality. The presumption of unity did not prevent Buddhist commentators, in their disputes, from putting competing accounts into opposition.[6] Nonetheless, the Three Turnings of the Wheel of Dharma,[7] taken together, constitutes a kind of road map for the route from *saṃsara* to *nirvāṇa* and *bodhi*, via emptiness, or suspension of judgment about beliefs.

The simplest terms for the Three Turnings may be Suffering, Emptiness, and *Bodhi*. The First Turning—as I hope to establish in this chapter—revolves around the recognition of suffering as related to dependent origination (*pratītya-samutpāda*), as expressed in the Buddha's first sermon at Sarnath; the Second Turning is the recognition of the emptiness of the phenomenal world, associated with the Buddha's discourses at Vulture Peak; the Third Turning is the reconciliation of the realization of tranquility or enlightenment or *bodhi*, which arises out of the resolution of dependent origination with emptiness. This understanding of the Turnings is most closely aligned with the findings of Lusthaus.

If *nirvāṇa* can be described as the release which follows the discovery of emptiness, then *bodhi* appears to be the state subsequent to that release, the condition which follows upon its achievement, no different, it seems, from the tranquility the Pyrrhonists call *ataraxia*. In the Buddhist literature, it was left to Nāgārjuna and the Mādhyamaka to articulate most persuasively the emptiness of all things, and to Vasubandhu and the Yogācāra to complete the reconciliation of emptiness with dependent origination, extinguishing all duality. They only presumed, of course, to represent what they were certain the Buddha had already discovered.

Finally, we will also explore the parallels between the Three Turnings of the Wheel of Dharma and the quadrilemma as reported in the Pyrrhonian tradition by Timon and Sextus.[8] A quadrilemma is a problem which has four (and only four) possible answers. The quadrilemma was also known in the earliest Buddhist texts we have, as well as among Greek philosophers, including Plato and Aristotle.[9] The first two steps of the quadrilemma—the assertion of a positive belief, followed by the opposing assertion of a negative belief (the contradiction of the former by the latter)—taken together present a dilemma, or an unavoidable binary choice. An assertion becomes problematic only when paired with its opposite to generate a dilemma. Dilemmas polarize their contents; they set up a choice between extremes. "God exists," one might assert, only to be opposed by the counter assertion, "God does not exist."

A dilemma is a sticking point, a linguistic obstruction which checks and distorts the flow of experience. A response to the challenge of dilemma is the subject of the First Turning, on impermanence and the Middle Way, as found in the Buddha's first sermon and related discourses. The Second Turning is a response, as we shall see, to trilemma, and the Third Turning to quadrilemma.

The subject of the First Turning—the release from the bondage of dilemma—is the recovery of the factual state of affairs the Buddha called dependent origination and the Pyrrhonists called appearances. Scholars, teachers, and commentators talk about the First Turning mostly in terms of the Four Noble Truths, the Eight-Fold Path, and so on, and not so much about dependent origination, but, as Lusthaus notes, quoted above, the First Turning rests upon "emphasizing entities (dharmas, aggregates, etc.)." which are dependently originated. This examination of the contents of consciousness, of immediate phenomena or thoughts and sensations, is all about overcoming our ignorance of dependent origination by focusing on what it is we directly experience. That process is geared to reestablish in the practitioner a recognition of dependent origination without which liberation from attachments, or beliefs, cannot be realized.

The central importance of dependent origination can hardly be overestimated. It is often called the heart of Buddhism: "Now this has been said by the Blessed One: 'One who sees dependent origination sees the Dhamma; one who sees the Dhamma sees dependent origination.'"[10] The explanation of the *dhamma* offered in the Buddhist scriptures is consistent, if not always clear. The classic formulation, variously embroidered in the sūtras, is given in the Buddha's first sermon at Sarnath, which revolves around what the *dhamma* is not. The Buddha begins by noting the duality of dilemma, of the "two extremes," which obscures dependent origination, and is to be overcome. This duality is presented as the pursuit of "sensual happiness" on the one hand, and the pursuit of "self-mortification" on the other. He advocates in its place the famous "middle way, which gives rise to vision, which gives rise to knowledge, which leads to peace, to direct knowledge, to enlightenment, to Nibanna." The steps along the middle way are the Four Noble Truths: the Noble Truth of Suffering; the Noble Truth of the origin of suffering; the Noble Truth of the cessation of suffering; and the Noble Truth of the path to the cessation of suffering. With this sermon, we are told, "the Wheel of the Dhamma had been set in motion by the Blessed One."[11]

Pragmata *and dependent origination* 71

A fuller account of duality, understood as dilemma, is given in the sutta *Kaccānagotta*, in the *Saṃyutta Nikāya*, as follows:

> This world, Kaccāna, for the most part depends upon a duality—upon the notion of existence and the notion of nonexistence. But for one who sees the origin of the world as it really is with correct wisdom, there is no notion of nonexistence in regard to the world. And for one who sees the cessation of the world as it really is with correct wisdom, there is no notion of existence in regard to the world....
>
> "All exists:" ... this is one extreme. "All does not exist:" this is the second extreme. Without veering toward either of these extremes, the Tathāgata teaches the Dhamma by the middle: "With ignorance as condition, volitional formations [come to be]; with volitional formations as condition, consciousness.... Such is the origin of this whole mass of suffering. But with the remainderless fading away and cessation of ignorance comes cessation of volitional formations, with the cessation of volitional formations, cessation of consciousness.... Such is the cessation of this whole mass of suffering."[12]

In this important and highly condensed passage, the Buddha outlines the Middle Path in terms of the obstacles faced by the practitioner, who aims to avoid "veering toward either of these extremes," towards either existence or non-existence. The "one who sees the origin of the world as it really is with correct wisdom," as the Buddha puts it, is one who sees dependent origination. It is our ignorance of dependent origination which allows us to imagine the independent origination of our experience, of our thoughts and sensations, and our own selves. It is to attribute to them some kind of inherent existence. The Buddhists propose to deconstruct our illusions of independent origination by resolving our experience back into dependent terms. We begin by considering that what we think are independently originated interpretations of our experience are in fact dependently originated.

Descriptions of dependent origination are found scattered throughout the several collections of *suttas*, including the early *Sutta Piaka*. Though sometimes varying in detail, they are highly consistent. The chief feature of experience exposed and disarmed by dependent origination is said to be *dukkha*, most commonly translated as suffering. The word means not only the involuntary presence of our thoughts and sensations insofar as we cannot help but experience them, but also that we suffer insofar as we fixate upon certain thoughts in particular by imagining that they reflect a permanent, independently existing feature of reality. It turns out that the latter blocks the dependent origination evident in the former, leaving us in ignorance of how things really are.

Dependent origination is the declared ontology and common legacy of early as well as normative Buddhism. It is not, however, like nearly all Western ontologies, a theory or abstraction or interpretation of experience. It is rather, like Pyrrhonian phenomenalism, a description of experience focused on what's taken to be indisputable evidence of impermanent elements as they are immediately present to consciousness—that is, our immediate thoughts and sensations, including the feelings (power, beauty, fear, etc.) associated with them.

Theodore Stcherbatsky, the pioneering Buddhist scholar writing a century ago, memorably described this as the consciousness of someone "to whom the universe presented itself as an infinite process of separate elements of matter and mind, appearing and disappearing, without any real personalities, nor any permanent substances."[13] The impermanence displayed by dependent origination is neither chaotic or random. The phenomena we directly experience turn out to be mutually conditioning, or co-dependent, often in predictable ways. Dependent origination is not a theory or interpretation of experience; it is instead a description of actual experience common to normal people under normal circumstances. Dependent origination was what the Buddhists understood as Right View, the first step on the eight-fold path. Before we can proceed further on the path, we need to understand, Buddhists maintain, the actual nature of experience as we experience it; we need to have the Right View, or *sammā diṭṭhi*. If *samma* means fulfilled or perfected, and *diṭṭhi* is our understanding, Right View is the correct understanding of how things actually are, which turns out to be dependent origination.

Right View is the middle path of co-dependency which steers between the two great errors or misunderstandings about experience: the dilemma of existence vs. non-existence, or Eternalism vs. Annihilationism, which nicely parallel the positive and negative dogmatisms of the Pyrrhonists. Eternalists, who are positive dogmatists, presume that the phenomena we experience are determined by something other than the phenomena themselves, by something existing independently of them which endures beneath the transient flux of phenomena, and somehow informs it. For the Eternalists the Buddha had in mind, the main independently existing thing to which they clung was the endlessly reincarnating Self, through which they believe the flux of experience flows. But the choice of a fixed, eternal thing can be other than the Self; it can also be God or Nature, or a Force, Substance, or Concept; it could be anything we might presume to be the nature or essence of any phenomenal display, or fact, in question, such as Beauty, or Evil, or Pleasure, etc. It could be as trivial as the Platonic form of "bed," or as expansive as the Platonic form of "justice." The Eternalist takes our phenomenal experience as displayed in *pragmata* not at face value, but as something which is not what it appears to be, something which stands in need of interpretation, something which can be pinned down and fixed in place.

The Annihilationists, in contrast to this, doubt the validity of all such interpretations, or concepts, or determining principles. They are negative dogmatists (like the Academics) decried by the Pyrrhonists, they see literally *nothing at all* behind the veil of impermanent appearances. In their view, there is no Love or Beauty, Evil or Justice, or any other essence behind phenomena. Such essences, they conclude, do not exist. Lacking any defining essence, the Annihilationists go on to conclude that appearances have no meaning at all. Any order among appearances is for them only contingent and arbitrary, an illusion at best.

The Middle Path of dependent origination, in contrast to the extremes of Eternalism and Annihilationism, accepts at face value the co-dependent appearance of phenomena, and makes no attempt at interpreting it. Instead, it takes note of the *pragmata*, or facts, displayed as forms by the appearances, or phenomena, that we actually experience. Some facts are unique (the sinking of the Titanic); others commonly recur (the water continuously going over Niagara Falls). But all are mutually defined by the phenomena which compose them, by their parts, as well as by the roles facts play in conjunction with other facts, the wholes in which they appear. They are neither independently determined as the Eternalists claim; nor are they illusions representing nothing as the Annihilationists insist.

Phenomena can be interpreted as illusions representing nothing only on the assumption that the only meaning they can have is as representations of independently existing entities, even though the latter cannot be found. Annihilationists accept the failure to demonstrate the independent existence underlying our thoughts and sensations, but nonetheless continue to presuppose its existence to make sense of *pragmata*, thus devaluing them as illusions. In this sense, Annihilationism is the shadow of Eternalism. The Middle

Path offers a contrasting description of the actual flow of phenomenal experience—the First Turning of the Wheel of *dhārmā*—which avoids these extremes. This turning of the wheel seeks to put into motion the flow of things as they come and go, freed of the interpretations which ensnare them: including the Eternalist belief in independently existing objects, and the Annihilationist belief in the non-existence of objects.

Dependent origination is introduced in the First Turning in the Pāli *suttas* as something hidden from us by our ignorance. Nonetheless, it remains the operative dynamic of our experience, proceeding in spite of our ignorance and suffering. Here's one of the most definitive and succinct statements found in the texts, which deserves close analysis:

> "And what, bhikkhus," asked the Buddha, "is dependent origination? With ignorance as condition, volitional formations [come to be]; with volitional formations as condition, consciousness; with consciousness as condition, name-and-form; with name-and-form as condition, the six sense-bases; with the six sense-basis as condition, contact; with contact as condition, feeling; with feeling as condition, craving; with craving as condition, clinging; with clinging as condition, existence; with existence as condition, birth; with birth as condition, aging-and-death, sorrow, lamentation, pain, displeasure, and despair come to be. Such is the origin of this whole mass of suffering. This, bhikkhus, is called dependent origination."[14]

This account of dependent origination begins with ignorance. And ignorance, we have been told, is displayed by Eternalists and the Annihilationists alike who conform respectively to the equally ignorant positive and negative dogmatists decried by the Pyrrhonists. Since this includes everyone not on the Middle Path, which is almost everybody, this is the logical place for the Buddha to begin his teaching. It is striking that the Buddhist trilogy of Eternalism, Annihilationism, and the Middle Path is paralleled by the Pyrrhonian distinction made by Sextus, on the very first page of his *Outlines*, between positive dogmatism, negative dogmatism, and the third way of Pyrrhonian scepticism, or science and inquiry. The Buddha too, by the way, describes the Middle Path as avoiding extremes, as one of inquiry: "[B]hikkhus, you should train thus: 'We shall be wise men; we shall be inquirers.'"[15]

Eternalism and Annihilationism are the two parallel errors which induce ignorance. The totalizing scepticism of the Annihilationists is a reaction to the disappointments which follow the Eternalist assertion of permanent entities, a retreat into cynicism and nihilism. As a result, both Eternalism and Annihilationism, like the positive and negative dogmatisms of the Pyrrhonists, divert our attention from the actual experience of dependent phenomena, and thereby place us in ignorance of it. In both cases we have a dilemma—Eternalism vs. Annihilationism, or positive vs. negative dogmatism—leaving us with the conclusion that neither can be shown to be the case.

Our ignorance, the Buddha is saying, is what leaves us free to imagine how things might be independently established (Eternalism) or not (Annihilationism). The sequence he describes turns on the exercise of the imagination, first evident in volitional formations; these produce a peculiar and fateful awareness—an ignorant or false consciousness of what the imagination can do. This false awareness encourages us to inflate our imagination, to presume that name and form, or signs, in fact represent independently existing things. This apparent ability to signify such things in turn becomes the condition of our projection of the six senses, that is, of what we take to be independently existing physical and mental worlds. This projection of our senses in turn allows us to imagine the senses (thoughts and sensations) to be *our* senses, that we are in contact with them as independently existing. The effect of this presumed possession produces positive, negative, or neutral effects, which become the condition of *our* feelings. Our feelings in turn become the condition of clinging to some of the things we imagine, and of our aversion or indifference to others. Clinging, aversion, and indifference in turn perpetuate our belief in the independent existence of objects we desire or avoid. The belief in the independent existence of such objects is the condition of karmic destiny, death, and rebirth, over and over again.

Central to this process is the power of the imagination. It is the imagination which seeks to fill the void of what is non-evident, and which creates through signification an array of non-evident objects, including a fictional Self, whose attractions and repulsions induce in us a belief in their independent existence, which entrains us to an endless karmic destiny, and which, given the continued operation of dependent origination, inevitably dissolves into impermanence and death. The recognition of this process is necessary to liberate us from the tyrannical illusion of our belief in independently existing objects, including our own identity as a Self. The assertion of independent existence/non-existence is possible, the text tells us, only out of ignorance of dependent origination. And liberation from ignorance presumes knowledge of dependent origination, which turns on the point of how ignorance can arise in the first place.

Let's examine the role of the imagination more carefully. The initial action, which opens the door to ignorance, is the creation of "volitional formations" (*saṇkhāra*). "*Saṇkhāra*," writes Bhikkhu Bodhi, the translator of the *Saṃyutta Nikāya*, "is derived from the prefix *sam* (=con), 'together,' and the verb *karoti*, 'to make.' The noun," he tells us, "straddles both sides of the active-passive divide."[16] We can understand *saṇkhāra* as the association of two or more otherwise discrete and separate phenomena which we ourselves are able to put together voluntarily in our imaginations, and also physically (as in gesture, speech, art, etc., by which we can represent what we first imagine mentally). The imagination, in other words, is what enables the very first step towards ignorance.

We can understand these volitional formations (or imaginative acts) by contrasting them with non-volitional formations. The latter, as we've seen, are the things we suffer involuntarily in the immediate flow of thoughts and sensations, and the patterns or *pragmata* they display, in which we are continuously entrained. It is only in our imaginations that we are largely if not wholly free of such involuntary constraints. Buddhists, like Pyrrhonists, see two kinds of suffering: the voluntary suffering induced by our imaginary constructs, or beliefs, which can be relieved, and the involuntary suffering of our dependently originated thoughts and sensations. Our minds (our imaginations), by contrast, are far freer to roam, seemingly without effort, than our bodies. It's far easier to imagine taking a hike in the woods than it is to actually take a hike in the woods. It is out of this strange power, the Buddha tells us, that we ultimately construct—out of ignorance—a self in which we imagine we find ourselves reflected. Any such volitional formation is above all a willful act of the imagination.

A "making together," a volitional formation, is a mental combination or association of things otherwise not so combined or associated. It is an association made by the human imagination, and the essential building block for constructing attachments or beliefs for both Buddhists and Pyrrhonists. When we imagine, or assert, that X is Y, we are saying that X isn't really what it seems to be, but in fact that it is something else, namely, Y, something quite different, some other fact or *pragma* which we presume exists. This is no more or less than the power of human imagination—of our ability to make mental identifications between otherwise unrelated items of experience.

Pragmata *and dependent origination* 77

This power of the human imagination makes possible the whole sequence of states of ignorance the Buddha enumerates. The Buddha, like Descartes, is telling us that we exist because we think. But each meant very different things by thinking. For Descartes thinking was abstraction, the draining away of content by greater and greater generalizations. For the Buddha, as well as the Pyrrhonists, thinking is not abstraction. It is our concrete phenomenal imagination at work, displayed by our mental images. We come to believe we exist because our ignorance of dependent origination allows us to imagine that we exist.

The dependent origination obscured by our ignorance turns out to be a phenomenalistic ontology, like the one developed by the Pyrrhonists, where the crucial distinction is between the evident (the involuntary direct objects of perception) and the non-evident (the interpretations of those objects by the imagination). Things evident cannot be denied; they involuntarily intrude on our consciousness. The Greek word in Sextus translated as "things" is *pragmata*, as we've seen, a notoriously broad and slippery term over which scholarly confusion continues to reign. In Liddell and Scott's Greek-English *Lexicon* possible meanings of *pragmata* include: deed, fact, matter, thing, necessity, consequence, circumstance, and affair, among others. Without a clear sense of what *pragmata* means, any account of Pyrrhonism (and early Buddhism) will remain vague.

Fortunately, evidence for the meaning of *pragmata* as dependently originated for the Pyrrhonists can be found in Sextus Empiricus.[17] In Sextus, as we've seen, our *pragmata* are the phenomena we directly experience, organized as thoughts and sensations. These phenomena are distinguished by their involuntary nature as experiences we can't help having when we have them. Sextus calls them "passive and unwilled feelings."[18] To reiterate an earlier point: I cannot help but see the blue sky outside on a sunny day if I have normal eyes to see. I cannot help but hear a chord I strike on my piano if I have normal ears to hear. And so on for the other senses. Similarly, I cannot help but think of my mother when I am thinking of her. My thoughts are what I remember and imagine—the mental pictures I project to myself, my memories, and ruminations. Insofar as early Buddhism can be understood to be expressed in Pyrrhonism, early Buddhists would have understood phenomena in the same way.

If we reimagine dependent origination in Pyrrhonian terms, we recognize that the phenomenal elements of our experience are *not* to be explained by reference to entities or forces existing separately and independently of those elements. The corresponding word for these elements, or phenomenal atoms, in Buddhism is *dharmas*—a term, if anything, even more elusive than *pragmata*. The commentaries on the Pali Canon, we're told on good authority, "... ascribe at least ten different contextual meanings to the word [*dharma*] as it occurs in the Canon...."[19] Normative Buddhism exemplifies this uncertainty with numerous lists of *dharmas*, including the well known list of 75 *dharmas* developed by the Sarvastivadins.[20]

What normative Buddhism seems to have done to come up with, say, 75 *dharmas*, is to consider sensations and thoughts not just in themselves, but also in a number of different relations or roles with one another. These include, in Buddhist language, *dharmas* that are inflows or outflows, internal or external, past, present, or future, etc. These *dharmas* are various different groups of phenomena, or *pragmata*. But, in all these variations, *dharmas* remain the immediate objects of perception present to consciousness: they are at bottom either sensations or thoughts. There is no *dharma* that is not a thought or a sensation.

The Buddhist classifications of various groups of *dharmas*—for instance, the *skandhas*—can be understood as functionally equivalent to the Pyrrhonian classifications of phenomena into the *pragmata*, or facts, which constitute our experience. The recognition that Democritean atomism could be shorn of its dogmatism and repurposed to accommodate Buddhist phenomenalism was, as proposed earlier, Pyrrho's defining achievement. The Buddhist contribution to this equation was the recognition that atoms, as well as the *pragmata* they display, are transient events in consciousness, without any independent invisible existence sustaining them in their absence from consciousness (as classical Democritean atomists believed). The atoms of Pyrrhonian Buddhism are neither eternal, nor non-existent, as far as we can tell, but they are recurring, and in that sense universals.

In Pyrrho's day, the detailed superstructure later established in the Pāli Canon, the Abhidharma, and other early Buddhist commentary, was almost certainly not fully articulated. In those early circumstances, it may have been less important which classifications of *dharmas*, or *pragmata*, were the most accurate, or the most helpful. What may have mattered more was the basic insight of the richness and complexity of the flow of *all* phenomena—however variously displayed as *skandhas/pragmata*—understood as the product of their mutual dependence. The appearing and disappearing world of phenomenal atomism is the world of things evident; the absence of phenomena is the non-evident. Early

Buddhism, insofar as we can reimagine it reflected in Pyrrhonism, may have been a simpler, more direct, more accessible practice of liberation from beliefs than later Buddhism.

What changes in our experience is not the phenomena themselves, which reliably recur, but the different facts into which these phenomena are variously combined. A phenomenal element is always recognizably the same whenever it appears—say, a certain shade of color, a certain tone of sound, a certain taste, and so on. But what it means will depend on the other phenomena with which it is invariably combined into one or another fact (*pragma* or *skandha*). Just as letters of the alphabet have no intrinsic meaning, but can be combined to express endless meanings in words, sentences, paragraphs, and entire texts, so phenomena in themselves have no intrinsic meaning (that is, no reference except self-reference), but, when variously combined into facts, they display an endless range of meanings.

Facts are dependently originated out of the phenomena which compose them. Such dependently originated facts, Sextus tells us, are the criteria by which a liberated Pyrrhonist tries to live—just as a Buddhist does. Our phenomena are recurring universals, but they are structured and given meaning by the various particular facts in which they appear, and which they constitute, impermanent as those facts may be. Without the appearance of facts, there is no coherence, no reliability, only chaos. A phenomenal gesture I experience—say, a raised hand—will have a different meaning depending on the context, or larger fact, in which it appears. It might, for instance, be a greeting in one case, a warning in another, a surrender in a third, a question in a fourth, and so on.

The appearance and disappearance of facts reflects the fundamental impermanence of the world of *dharma*, of *pragmata*. In the Right View of things, that is, in the natural operation of dependent origination, the *pragmata* which arise out of co-dependent phenomena are in constant flux. We recognize not only the occurrence and recurrence of distinct *pragmata*, but also the changes which transform them over time. The oil painting I see today in my living room, for instance, is virtually indistinguishable, as far as I can tell, from what it was when I looked at it yesterday, under similar conditions. By contrast, this evening's sunset may differ subtly from yesterday's, even if it still reminds me of it. The variations of recombinant, co-determinate phenomena are virtually endless, at least as endless as what can be imagined, or spoken.

But this flux is not chaos. The flow of *pragmata* is neither random nor incomprehensible. There are anomalies, surprises, and catastrophes in our experience, to be sure, but much if not most of what flows through us makes up the reliable round of events associated with everyday life. Pyrrhonism and Buddhism both recognize that knowledge is to had, not about the objects of belief, but about our experience of *pragmata*, our physical and mental nature. Pyrrhonian Buddhism allows for a phenomenological science of natural experience, of the *dharma*. In Pyrrhonian language, it's the phenomenalistic ontology embodied in Sextus' Methodist medical practice, where apparent phenomena are the criterion of evidence.

Theodore Stcherbatsky's striking summary account of Buddhist *dharmas* was an important, if incomplete, first approximation in Western thinking about Buddhism as a phenomenalistic atomistic ontology, with recurring elements combined into changing facts. As he put it:

> The elements of existence [in Buddhism] are momentary appearances, momentary flashings into the phenomenal world out of an unknown source. Just as they are disconnected, so to say, in breadth, not being linked together by any pervading substance, just so they are disconnected in depth or in duration since they last only one single moment (*kṣaṇa*). They disappear as soon as they appear, in order to be followed the next moment by another momentary existence. Thus a moment becomes a synonym of an element (*dharma*), two moments are two different elements. An element becomes something like a point in time-space.... The idea that two moments make two different elements remains. Consequently, the elements do not change, but disappear, the world becomes a cinema. Disappearance is the very essence of existence; what does not disappear does not exist. A cause for the Buddhist was not a real cause but a preceding moment, which likewise arose out of nothing in order to disappear into nothing.[21]

Stcherbatsky goes on to further describe the Buddhist phenomenalistic ontology this way:

> The world was thus transformed into a cinema. The categories of substance, quality, and motion—for momentary flashes could possess no motion—were denied but the reality of sense data and of the elements of mind was admitted. All these elementary data were conceived as obeying causal laws. But the conception of causality was adapted to the character of these entities which

could neither change nor move, but could only appear and disappear. Causation was called dependently-coordinated origination (*pratītya-samutpāda*), or dependent existence. The meaning of it was that every momentary entity sprang into existence, or flashed up, in coordination with other moments. Its formula was "if there is this, there appears that."[22]

In sum, the theory of independent origination central to the First Turning, as we have it in the Buddhist texts, is a compressed account of two different things: first, an account of how dependent origination is obscured, resulting in entrapment and suffering in the pursuit of the illusion of permanence, and second, a phenomenalistic ontology, which appears to be presupposed but is never clearly described in the Buddhist texts.

The idea of a Buddhist phenomenalistic ontology, though not under that label, has been explored recently by Mark Siderits in an important work, *Buddhism as Philosophy*. As Siderits warns us, the idea of phenomenalistic ontology, that "there are no substances, only qualities, takes some getting used to."[23] Buddhists, like Pyrrhonists, as he reminds us, find no reason to postulate substances. Those are the independently existing essences of things favored by those the Buddhists called Eternalists, and the Pyrrhonists call Dogmatists, or people who hold beliefs, whether positive or negative.

Siderits struggles to clarify what the phenomenalistic atomism of Buddhism looks like. The difficulty is that the *dharmas* outlined in Abhidharma literature present no clear picture of the elements or atoms presumed to constitute our direct immediate experience, variously arranged into the *pragmata* they display. "It is important to remember," as a standard authority such as the *Stanford Encyclopedia of Philosophy* reminds us, "... that the term *dharma* signifies both any category that represents a type of occurrence as well as any of its particular tokens or instances."[24]

Reflecting this confusion between type and token, Siderits tells us that:

> it is difficult to explain the relation between atoms of the four elements [earth, air, fire, and water—a staple of Abhidharma analysis] on the one hand, and sensible properties like color and odor on the other, if both are ultimately real. For there is the fact that the sensible qualities like color are said to depend on the atoms

[earth, air, fire, and water], which makes the former seem less real than the latter. And there is also the fact that atoms are never themselves perceived but only inferred, whereas sensible qualities like color are directly perceived. Someone of an empiricist bent might conclude from this that atoms are conceptually constructed, and only sensible property-particulars are ultimately real.[25]

This last point was, I suggest, precisely the conclusion drawn by ancient Pyrrhonists and early Buddhists. No matter how the *dharmas* listed by various normative schools came to be distinguished—in some accounts numbering in the hundreds—they nonetheless all remain various arrangements of actual thoughts and sensations. As Siderits makes clear, the relevant distinction is between what is "conceptually constructed" and what is not. This can also be described as the distinction between what is inferred and what is perceived, or between what is non-evident and what is evident. And since it is thoughts and sensations which are perceived, not inferred, it is they which are our phenomenal *dharmas*. Siderits' presumption that "atoms are never themselves perceived but only inferred" reflects the original Democritean view, not the revised version of Pyrrho in which atoms are indeed perceived, even as they remain in flux. Better, in fact, to abandon the word "perception," with its implications of a determining process, in favor of the simple actuality of phenomena.

Siderits wrestles, as did Stcherbatsky, with how it is that phenomena, which exist only momentarily in consciousness, can nonetheless display the continuity they do. The question becomes pressing once we are faced, as he puts it, with

> the problem of explaining continuities among our dispositions in the absence of an enduring mind. For instance, I may retain the ability to speak a language I have not used for years. Put in the right environment, I suddenly find myself understanding and speaking it again. How is this to be explained if there is no enduring substance, the mind, in which that ability is lodged? The Sautrantika answer is that our actions create mental *dharmas* called "seeds." These replicate themselves in the mental stream until such time as conditions cause them to ripen. The ripening of a seed then brings about the appropriate mental event, such as understanding the word I just heard.[26]

Siderits' question, and the Sautrantika's answer, can only arise on the assumption that our *dharmas*, our immediate thoughts and sensations, are particulars—a staple of most philosophical thinking, East and West. If that is so, the job of linking them together, of sustaining their continuity, must be done by something else. Whatever achieves this for our *dharmas* resolves their particularity into some kind of universality, thereby unifying otherwise discrete appearances into a single thing. But if the traditional conceptual mechanism for drawing this conclusion is disqualified, then it seems we are left without any way to understand the continuities evidently displayed in our experience.

This is not a problem for Pyrrhonism Buddhism. In its understanding, as this work tries to demonstrate, things are quite otherwise: our *dharmas*, understood as our phenomenal elements, evidently recur precisely because they are universals, not particulars. We literally recognize them as they reappear not because we have some mechanism for doing so but *because they actually reappear*. The assumption behind the interpretation of *dharmas* as particulars is, according to most of Western philosophy at least, that they lack numerical identity. "[P]roperties may be shared between two things," as Siderits puts it, "whereas numerical identity may not. The leaf on this branch of this tree today might be exactly like the leaf that was here last year—same color, same shape, same pattern of veins, etc. But they are numerically distinct leaves all the same."[27] It follows for Siderits, as it has for 'normative' Western philosophy, as well as for most of normative Buddhism, that anything we can perceive—any fact, or *pragma*—cannot be presumed to be identical with any earlier apparent manifestation, even if that appears to be the case.

Pyrrhonian Buddhism, by contrast, sees no need to question the apparent recurrence of our *dharmas* as the elements of the *pragmata* we perceive. When I reach for my coffee mug every morning, I have no reason to doubt that the mug I see and grasp is the same mug I saw and grasped yesterday. I could be wrong about this, it is true. Say it happens that there are two mugs on the shelf which are virtually identical—stamped from the same mold, let's say, which share, as far as I or anyone can tell, the same apparent qualities, without exception. In which case anyone could easily confuse the two. But this error, or confusion, is what actually proves what identity is. It shows the true nature of identity to be consistent with being plural, with recurrence, as our ordinary experience in fact testifies. For all practical (not theoretical) purposes, objects which have qualitative identity have actual identity. They do *not* need numerical identity to have actual (or interchangeable) identity. They are identical objects, perhaps as mundane as two identical coins in my pocket, or as esoteric as two particles in quantum physics, which can co-exist in more than one place at one time.

The fact that there can be numerically different but otherwise identical things is familiar enough in ordinary experience, from identical twins to identical drops of water to identical ceramic cups, to multiples of these, such as exact copies or replicas, and so on. We can hardly conclude otherwise if we take seriously the Pyrrhonian claim to distinguish appearances *qua* appearances (which are literally self-evident), from interpretations of appearances (which are not). The Pyrrhonian-Buddhist point is that numerical distinction clarifies rather than obscures the identity of objects. The supposition that numerical identity be among the criteria of identity is a conceptual construct, not an actual perception, and as such it is an obstacle, not a vehicle, to the recognition of the actual identity as presented in our direct experience. The suspension of numerical identity is akin, perhaps, to the suspension of Euclid's Fifth Postulate, on parallel lines; in both cases, a different reality emerges from what has been hitherto almost universally presupposed.

Recognizing what we variously call qualities, *dharmas*, elements, or atoms as interchangeable names for the same phenomenal universals—our immediate thoughts and sensations—makes it possible to see how facts or *pragmata*, including all the categories of *dharmas* (the *skandhas*, the conditioned and unconditioned *dharmas*, *karmic* patterns, and so on) are constructed out of them. *Pragmata* turn out to be the particulars constituted by combinations of phenomenal universals. Particulars can change, but the phenomena which constitute them do not change, even as they come and go.

Without the recognition of phenomena as recurring universals, the Middle Path could not be sustained. The inquirer sceptical of positive dogmatism would be driven into negative dogmatism, or Annihilationism. Here we find perhaps the deepest distinction between Pyrrhonian and normative Buddhism. As many have sensed—most prominently Nietzsche—normative Buddhism can easily slide into nihilism, as the Madhyamaka were accused of doing by the Yogacara. Nietzsche didn't say why, but we can see that this can happen insofar as we blur the line between interpretations of perceived phenomena and those phenomena in themselves—a view embraced by Nietzsche, and developed by his twentieth-century deconstructionist followers.

The Pyrrhonists by contrast take seriously the testimony of appearances; they cease to judge appearances or *pragmata* by the interpretations of them that can be offered. If it appears that phenomena recur, and (as in the example of the cup) that the *pragmata* they constitute recur as well, singularly or plurally, then we are obliged, if we follow appearances, rather than interpretations of appearances, to accept the recurrence of phenomena at face value.

It is as phenomena that *dharmas* have their own intrinsic nature. Siderits puts it this way: "To say that *dharmas* have intrinsic natures is to say that their natures are entirely their own, not borrowed. What this means is that something's being the *dharma* it is does not disappear under analysis. If it is something physical, it continues to be the kind of thing it is when we take away bits of it. It is also not capable of being conceptually analyzed into a plurality of distinct properties. We know we have reached *dharmas* when we have arrived at existence that cannot be reduced to other sorts of things. One way we might put this is to say that *dharmas* can only be known by acquaintance, not by description. That is, we could come to know what is meant by the name for a certain kind of *dharma* only through having direct experience of it."[28] Nonetheless, for Siderits, as quoted earlier, it is a "fact that atoms are never themselves perceived but only inferred." This prevents him from recognizing that, for the Pyrrhonian Buddhist, the "direct experience" of *dharma* is exactly the direct experience of phenomenal thoughts and sensations as arranged in an endless variety of facts, or *pragmata*. It is these which are known by acquaintance, not description, or interpretation.

A further clarification may be useful. *Dharmas* and the *pragmata* they combine to produce stand to one another, in our acquaintance of them as involuntarily experienced phenomena, as parts and wholes. And since parts and wholes nest within one another, a whole made of its own parts can also be a part of a larger whole, and so on. And, as far down as we can go in the other direction, at the very perceptual bottom, so to speak, we approach the phenomenal atoms we immediately and directly perceive. At that threshold, however, the atoms themselves disappear. Our phenomenal atoms are the recurring parts of the otherwise changing things (*pragmata*) which we know by virtue of their display by our immediate thoughts and sensations. The wholes constituted by our phenomenal atoms are apparent only as a display (some combination) of those original parts. As we ascend, going the other way, up, from the smallest *dharmas* we directly experience, we find that the immediate *pragmata* they constitute also play the role of parts in still larger wholes, or more inclusive *pragmata*, and so on. At the top of this process, at the limit of the horizon of consciousness, so to speak, the whole that is constituted (say the universe) does not find (at least not yet) a still larger whole in which to be a part, and so it too disappears. It remains no more than a limit, lacking any further contextual determination. This rounds off the top and bottom, so to speak, of the range of phenomenal display.

The wholes displayed by their parts, no matter the level, have no independent existence. There is only the dependent existence of wholes on the parts that display them. Parts themselves, even down to atoms, exist only in relation to other parts. But, throughout the nesting sequences of parts and wholes, it is always the recurring atoms—the phenomenal *dharmas* of thoughts and sensations—which continue to appear, or literally shine through, in any and all of the possible combinations and recombinations in which they are found. Even the largest and most comprehensive wholes—such as the universe—remain no more than vast complexes of *dharmas*, or thoughts and sensations, arranged in certain ways. At any level, the direct simplicity of immediate perception is always apparent. Even the most complex *pragmata* can be perceived at all only insofar as their display continues to depend on the immediately perceived phenomenal *dharmas* which are their parts.

The Buddha understood any phenomenal element as simply "this," or the immediate, direct, involuntary experience of a thought or sensation, as the Pyrrhonian texts suggest he might have. But the earliest Buddhist texts, unlike the Pyrrhonian literature, are not clear on this point. We have seen Siderits, like others, struggle under the assumption that phenomena must be particulars, not universals, and that therefore some kind of projection is required to underwrite the organization of particulars into classes or universals. This makes it effectively impossible to distinguish between phenomena and the *pragmata* they display.

Other Buddhist scholars writing about phenomenalism, such as Dan Lusthaus, fall victim to the same assumption. Lusthaus' lengthy and exhaustive study, *Buddhist Phenomenalism*, is at pains to show that Yogācāra phenomenology in particular is not a form of subjective idealism.[29] The model of phenomenology Lusthaus invokes is not Pyrrhonian, however, but that of Husserl and his followers. This is not the place to analyze Husserlian phenomenology, but it too struggles to distinguish particular phenomena from organizational, non-phenomenal concepts. It is hardly a model for the phenomenalistic ontology of Pyrrhonian Buddhism.

Of course, we find this confusion of phenomena with particulars in Buddhist literature as well. The Buddha's observation that nothing is permanent, if we read it in Pyrrhonian terms, is the observation that no fact (no *pragma*, *dharma*, or *skandha*—nothing we might recognize as an object of any sort, mental or physical) is permanent. But that is no reason to suppose that the phenomena themselves, although they are coming and going, are themselves impermanent. The Buddha's silence about ontological questions was not respected by all of his followers, some of whom ended up in the same speculative confusion. In their presumption that momentarily experienced phenomena were particulars—a view the Buddha would have eschewed as speculative—later Buddhist philosophers had to explain the coherence and continuity of experience. Their best known effort, that of the Sautrantikas, postulated the existence of mental *dharmas* they called "seeds," which ripened under the right circumstances, tying together past and present experiences. But none of this is an issue in Pyrrhonian Buddhism, where the universality of mental and physical phenomena is taken as self-evident.

The middle path presented in the First Turning is pursued by suspending judgment regarding extremes, that is, dogmatic beliefs. For Pyrrhonists (and early Buddhists) such judgments are signs, where something is used to represent something else, and the only issue is whether an actual referent for what is presumed to be a sign can be found. Those for which referents can be found, Sextus calls recollective (or commemorative signs), and those for which referents cannot be found, he calls indicative signs. In his words in the *Outlines*:

> There being two different sorts of signs ... we argue not against all signs but only against indicative signs, which seem to be a fiction of the Dogmatists. For recollective signs are found convincing by everyday life: seeing smoke, someone diagnoses fire; having observed a scar, he says that a wound was inflicted. Hence not only do we not conflict with everyday life, but we actually join the struggle on its side, assenting without opinion to what it has found convincing and taking a stand against the private fictions of the Dogmatists.[30]

The Dogmatists (Eternalists and Annihilationists in Buddhist terms) assert the real existence, or non-existence, of the referents of the "indicative" signs they imagine to exist, even though they cannot actually produce those referents. As long as these "indicative" signs, or fictions, remain unverified by any convincing referent, they can easily be denied: If we assert "man is immortal," we invite the response "man is not immortal." If we assert "man is a wolf," we not only invite the response "man is not a wolf," but also responses such as "man is a snake," or "man is a god," or any number of other competing judgments. If immortal-men and wolf-men and snake-men and god-men and other similar X-men can equally be imagined and denied, then none can have a special claim to exist, barring their actual appearance in our sensory experience.

In their mutual opposition, such judgments cancel one another out, and it is Pyrrhonian practice, as catalogued in the modes, to articulate these oppositions and set them against one another. Sextus describes the technique of opposing views this way: "Scepticism is an ability to set out oppositions among things which appear and are thought of in any way at all, an ability by which, because of the equipollence in the opposed objects and accounts, we come first to suspension of judgment and afterwards to tranquility."[31]

Suspension of judgment is achieved, as Sextus tells us, "through the opposition of things." He sums it up this way: "we oppose what appears to what appears, or what is thought of to what is thought of, or crosswise."[32] In this way we reach equipollence, or a balance of power among judgments. Judgment is suspended when it becomes evident that the sides opposed to one another have equal plausibility, and no side is able to "win" (or "lose") any argument. The suspension of judgment, as we shall see in the next chapter, leads to what the Buddhists call the emptiness of the things being judged, to a recognition of their lack of content, which is the precondition of tranquility.

This dynamic of opposition might be illustrated as follows: If there are strong communities of immortal-men believers, for instance, or wolf-men believers, or snake-men believers, or god-men believers, and so on, and if there are also communities of sceptics who outright deny immortal men, wolf-men, snake-men, and god-men, and so on, then there will not be tranquility. There will be disputation, not only between believers and sceptics, but among the different believers. There is no apparent way to resolve such disputes, which, left unchecked, tend towards conflict and violence. That the existence of immortal-men (or wolf-men, snake-men, god-men, etc.) can neither be proven nor disproven is evident, according to both Pyrrhonism and Buddhism, by the absence of confirming phenomenal evidence, by their lack of phenomenal realization, by their emptiness.

Such beliefs are necessarily speculative; they might or might not turn out to apply to experience, and we have no way of knowing whether they can or not as long as no referents for them can be found. They turn us, insofar as we believe them, into gamblers, rolling the dice, betting on some of them as if they were true, and others false. We gamble with many beliefs, including our religious and ideological beliefs about God, Soul, Race, History, Nation, Freedom, Gender, Party, Nature, Truth, Justice, Rights, Markets, and many, many others. These are among our most fundamental attachments, and it is from their burden that Pyrrhonian Buddhism seeks to relieve us by demonstrating their emptiness, or absence. The life of the Pyrrhonian Buddhist is a life without beliefs, a life empty of beliefs.[33]

In Pyrrhonian Buddhism, the natural flow of dependent origination is disrupted by attempts to signify what cannot be signified: what Sextus called the naturally non-evident. I can imagine a centaur, or mermaid, or Santa Claus, or Sherlock Holmes, or any number of fictional characters and narratives, as expressed in stories, novels, epics, or myths, and so on. Once we have experienced such imaginative *pragmata*, or myths, in our minds, it is but a short step to concluding that they signify something, that they are somehow representations of things non-evident with which, out of our ignorance of dependent origination, we are tempted to identify. I first have to be able to *imagine* that Jesus was the Son of God; only after that am I in a position to *believe* that he actually was the Son of God. Similarly, I first have to be able to *imagine* an "invisible hand" guiding individual self-interest in the marketplace to benefit society as a whole; only after that am I able to *believe* that individual self-interest automatically transfers into public good. And so on.

A thought, once imagined, remains available to the mind in memory as a more or less reliable *pragma* that usually can be called up at will. It's easy to slide into the belief that such a thought represents something existing outside of its own expression, outside of the mind, something independent and permanent, which the mental image represents. Belief creates the force (if not the reality) of truth through the pretense that it represents something. The effect is to freeze up our experience, to dam up what would otherwise be a freely flowing stream of *pragmata* by fixating on a static illusion believed to underlie that stream. A belief asserts a reality, even though that reality can neither be confirmed nor disconfirmed. As Sextus Empiricus puts it: "... if you hold beliefs, then you posit as real the things you are said to hold beliefs about...."[34]

Most beliefs led us into what the Buddhists call Eternalism, and what the Pyrrhonists call positive dogmatism. A false consciousness arises—a consciousness of pseudo-objects which are projected in imagination, and then fixated by belief; they are sustained by the misrepresentation of trying to signify what is non-evident. Central to the pseudo-signification that sustains belief is what Buddhists call name-and-form, or *nāma-rūpa*. Once we employ signification to falsely represent naturally non-evident things, we discover the power of projection to create nearly endless fictions from which we can pick our beliefs. The dogmatic Eternalist lives mostly in his or her mind, in a fantasy world superimposed on the actual world. Annihilationists too live mostly in their minds, obsessed, in their negative dogmatism, with something different: with the failure to establish the convincing beliefs they still believe ought to be established to make sense of things.

We cling to our beliefs, or dogmas, all the more fervently as others challenge them. Perturbed and distressed at the conflicts which ensue, we tend to double down on our beliefs, or replace them with what we hope are better beliefs, which are in turn open to challenge, and so on. This is the struggle with dilemma that dependent origination is invoked to resolve in the First Turning. We give our beliefs an artificial injection of reality by pumping them up through conviction or intuition, precisely because we are unable to support them empirically. This is the point where belief slides into dogma, where issues are no longer debated, only repeated. The dogmatist can abandon one belief in favor of another, to be sure, but this only perpetuates the cycle. He or she can also adopt the alternate view of the Annihilationists, and reject all beliefs. But having no beliefs is as much a belief as having a specific belief. So here too the cycle plays itself out.

Notes

1 *Wisdom of Buddha: The Saṃdhinirmocana Sūtra*, trans. John Powers (Berkeley: Dharma) 139–45.
2 Jay L. Garfield, "The Three Turnings of the Wheel of Dharma: Why They Are Each Essential to All of Us," *Tibetan Buddhism in the West: Problems of Adoption and Cross-Cultural Confusion*, Berlin: Public Talk, 2011, https://info-buddhism.com/Three_Turnings_of_The_Wheel_of_Dharma_Jay_Garfield.html.
3 James Blumenthal, "Three Turnings of the Wheel of Dharma," *Mandala*, October–December, 2008 18–19.
4 Tenshin Reb Anderson, "Why the Wheel Turns Three Times," *Lion's Roar*, 14 May 2012, https://www.lionsroar.com/why-the-wheel-turns-three-times/.
5 Dan Lusthaus, "What Is and Isn't Yogācāra," *Yogācāra Buddhism Research Association*, 2, http://www.acmuller.net/yogacara/articles/intro.html.
6 See, for example, Dan Lusthaus, "The Heart Sūtra in Chinese Yogācāra: Some Comparative Comments on the Heart Sūtra Commentaries," *International Journal of Buddhist Thought and Culture* 3 (2003) 66–7; https://www.academia.edu/225330/The_Heart_S%C5%ABtra_in_Chinese_Yog%C4%81c%C4%81ra_Some_Comparative_Comments_on_the_Heart_S%C5%ABtra_Commentaries_of_W%C5%8Fnch%C5%ADk_and_Kuei-chi?email_work_card=view-paper.
7 I use *dharma* rather than *dḥārṃā* throughout as this Sanskrit term has become normalized as an English word.
8 See Empiricus, *Outlines of Scepticism.*, op. cit., I, xx, 47–8, where the quadrilemma is strongly implied as "non-assertion in the general sense," i.e., including positive and negative assertions.

Pragmata *and dependent origination* 91

9 See Plato's *Republic*, 479c4–5 and Aristotle's *Metaphysics*, T1008a.
10 *Majjhima* Nikāya, I, 190–1, in *The Middle Length Discourses of the Buddha: A Translation of the Majjhima Nikāya*, trans. Bhikhu Nanamoli and Bhikku Bodhi (Boston, MA: Wisdom Publications, 3rd ed., 2005) 284.
11 *Saṃyuta Nikaya*, V, 56, 11, in *The Connected Discourses of the Buddha: A Translation of the Saṃyuta Nikaya*, trans. Bhikku Bodhi (Boston, MA: Wisdom Publications, 2000) 1843–7.
12 Ibid., 544.
13 Theodore Stcherebatsky, *The Conception of Buddhist Nirvana* (New York: Samuel Weiser, 2nd ed., 1978) 3.
14 *Samyuta Nikaya*, II, 1.1, in *The Connected Discourses of the Buddha: A Translation of the Samyuta Nikaya*, trans. Bhikku Bodhi (Boston, MA: Wisdom Publications, 2000) 533.
15 *Majjhima Nikaya*, III, 115.2, in *The Middle Length Discourses of the Buddha: A Translation of the Majjhima Nikaya*, trans. Bhikkhu Nanamoli and Bhikkhu Bodhi (Boston, MA: Wisdom Publications, 3rd ed., 2005) 925.
16 "Introduction" to *The Connected Discourses of the Buddha: A Translation of the Saṃyuta Nikaya*, trans. Bhikku Bodhi (Boston, MA: Wisdom Publications, 2000) 45.
17 Beckwith maintains that Sextus "hardly deviates *systematically* in any significant way from Early Pyrrhonism," Beckwith, op. cit., 20.
18 Empiricus, *Outlines of Scepticism*, op. cit., 9.
19 Bhikkhu Bodhi, "Introduction" in *The Middle Length Discourses of the Buddha: A Translation of the Majjhima Nikāya*, trans. Bhikkhu Nanamoli and Bhikkhu Bodhi (Boston, MA: Wisdom Publications, 2005) 54.
20 For a detailed listing, see Th. Stcherbatsky, *The Central Conception of Buddhism and the Meaning of the Word Dharma* (Delhi: Motilal Banarsidass Publishers, 2018 [1922], Appendix II, "Tables of the elements according to the Sarvastivadins," 93–107.
21 Ibid., 37–8.
22 Stcherbatsky, op. cit., 46.
23 Mark Siderits, *Buddhism as Philosophy: An Introduction* (Indianapolis: Hackett Publishing, 2007) 114.
24 "Abhidharma" in the *Stanford Encyclopedia of Philosophy*, https://plato.stanford.edu/entries/abhidharma/.
25 Siderits, op. cit., 117.
26 Ibid., 118.
27 Ibid., 34.
28 Ibid., 113.
29 Dan Lusthaus, *Buddhist Phenomenalism: A Philosophical Investigation of Yogācāra Buddhism and the Ch'eng Wei-shih lun* (New York: Routledge/Curzon, 2003).
30 Empiricus, op. cit., II, 93, 102.
31 Ibid., I, 4, 8.
32 Ibid., I, 31.
33 See Batchelor, op. cit., *et. passim*.
34 Empiricus, op. cit., 6.

6 Emptiness and the suspension of belief

Relief from beliefs, according to Pyrrhonian Buddhism, comes from suspending judgments about them, neither affirming nor denying them, but rather maintaining a silence—an emptiness—about them, just as the Buddha famously did. This is the Second Turning, the entry into the emptiness of things—into the recognition that the beliefs we hold about things non-evident remain empty insofar as they remain non-evident.

The flux of *pragmata*, their coming into being and passing away, obliges us to confront absence, or emptiness, as well as presence. The absence of a fact is as evident as its presence. Just as I cannot help but notice the students who come to class, if I'm paying attention, so I cannot help but notice when one of them fails to come to class. The absence of phenomena is just as self-evident as their presence. The Pyrrhonists, like the Buddhists, point out that the self, or soul, as they call it, nowhere appears as a phenomenal fact (as David Hume observed). The self, it seems, can only be an absence.

Pyrrhonists and early Buddhists noted only the absence of the self or soul; they resisted the speculative conclusion of its existence, or non-existence. They neither affirmed nor denied the soul, or self, but rather suspended judgment about it, leaving it wholly indeterminate. The Pyrrhonian soul is no more or less than an indeterminate subject to which, it seems, determinate phenomenal facts, or *pragmata*, are displayed. The indeterminate remains potentially determinate—but, in the meantime, uncertain and unpredictable. This suspension of belief in a determinate self, as well in as no self at all, leaving only an indeterminate self, would have been the early Buddhist understanding of the lack of a self, based on what Pyrrhonism tells us. The Buddhist school of *Pudgalavādins* was one sect which described a similar state, arguably in continuation of early Buddhism.[1]

If we combine the Pyrrhonian recognition of absence with the Buddhist recognition of emptiness, we get a distillation in which both are fused, and their distracting accretions are vented away. In both traditions, we have a meta-logical movement from the classic dilemma (X is Y vs. X is not Y) to the trilemma (X is neither Y nor not Y), which brings us to a point of suspension of judgment. This is the move from the First to the Second Turning. To say that X is neither Y nor not Y is to refrain from making either the judgment that X is Y, or the judgment that X is not Y. In this opposition, the emptiness of both Y and not Y, ultimately of existence and non-existence, is revealed.

Just as the Theravadan Pali scriptures and other early writings are the foundational texts of the First Turning on dependent origination, so the *Perfection of Wisdom* or *prajñāpāramitā sūtras* are the foundational texts of the Second Turning, on emptiness. Here too we find a written record, purportedly of words spoken or authorized by the Buddha, but also dating from hundreds of years later. What is interesting is not so much the question of chronology, however, but the meta-logical unfolding of the insights of the First Turning in the subsequent Turnings, beginning with their transformation into the Second Turning. One measure of authenticity is whether a text draws out the implications of what has already been stated, and that is very arguably the case here.

In the *Heart Sutra*, a brief compression of the thousands of lines of the *Perfection of Wisdom*, the Second Turning is famously summed up:

> Form is emptiness; emptiness is form. Emptiness is not other than form. Form also is not other than emptiness. Likewise, feeling, discrimination, compositional factors and consciousness are empty ... all phenomena are merely empty, having no characteristics. They are not produced and do not cease. They have no defilement and no separation from defilement. They have no decrease and no increase.[2]

The opposite of emptiness, for the Buddhists, is essence, or substance, some kind of fullness. The Sanskrit term for emptiness is *śūnyatā*; the term for essence or substance is *svabhāva*. The insight of emptiness is that the things we perceive—the forms displayed to us through our sensations and thoughts in *pragmata*—have no substance, no independent existence, apart from the experience we have of them as we experience them. We know them by acquaintance, not by inference. The empty forms of the Buddhists are precisely what the Pyrrhonists see displayed in *pragmata* by phenomena which appear relative to one another, or dependently originated. The forms displayed by *Pragmata* have no independent existence; they are displayed only by recurring phenomena, which "are not produced and do not cease." They too are empty of any essence.

Pragmata are available to us only insofar as they are displayed to us by the phenomena we involuntarily experience in sensation or thought. The forms they display are empty (*śūnyatā*) because they have no substance (*svabhāva*) apart from the phenomena from which they cannot be separated. Just as there is a convergence between Greek *pragmata* and Buddhist forms like the *skandhas*, so there is a convergence between Greek phenomena and the most elementary of Buddhist *dharmas*. Phenomena/*dharmas* are the discrete elements of sensation and thought which are endlessly combined and recombined to constitute *pragmata*/forms. This is, as outlined in the last chapter, the atomistic phenomenalistic ontology of Pyrrhonian Buddhism.

This phenomenalistic ontology is not to be confused with traditional philosophical beliefs supporting the independent existence of an external world, nor, by the same token, that of an internal or solipsistic world. For Pyrrhonian Buddhism, there is *only* a phenomenal world of thoughts and sensations (neither external nor internal) displaying a series of changing "empty" objects—the forms displayed by *pragmata* in consciousness. The forms (*pragmata*) have no independent reality, but are wholly conditioned by the phenomena which display them, much as the motion picture we see and hear is wholly dependent on the sights and sounds combined to display it in a theater or on a monitor.

What the Second Turning adds to the First Turning is the pervasive realization of emptiness, or absence, of any and all the forms displayed by the *pragmata* by which we live. In the First Turning, individual suffering is the focus; it is understood as arising from the loss of consciousness of dependent origination, of the fall into ignorance; the cessation of suffering occurs only with the recovery of consciousness of dependent origination, or knowledge. The mechanism of the First Turning, of ignorance, turns on the duality of dilemma, of the opposition of extremes, overcome in the recognition, in the Middle Path, of dependent origination. The focus is on the liberation of the individual, and the prototype is the *arhat*, who has overcome suffering and achieved *nirvana*. The Second Turning reveals the dependent origination of the whole world—as experienced by sentient beings—emptied of any independent existence, or non-existence. The mechanism here is the resolution of dilemma into trilemma, into a suspension of judgment about both the existence or non-existence of things. The focus moves from personal to cosmic enlightenment, or *bodhi*, and the prototype is the *bodhisattva*, the liberated individual dedicated to the liberation of all.

In Pyrrhonian practice, dependent origination is obscured to the extent to which one holds beliefs about non-evident things. This is closely paralleled by the Buddha's famous refusal to engage in metaphysical speculation—most notably in the so-called "unanswered questions." These are outlined most notably in a couple of suttas of the *Majjhima Nikāya*. In the "Sabbasava Sutta," on "All the Taints," the Buddha distinguishes between unwise attention and wise attention, between seeing and knowing and not seeing and knowing, between the facts of actual experience and what we imagine about those facts. As the Buddha put it:

> By attending to things unfit for attention and by not attending to things fit for attention, both arisen taints arise in him [he who is in ignorance] and arisen taints increase. This is how he attends unwisely: "Was I in the past? Was I not in the past? What was I in the past? How was I in the past? Having been what, what did I become in the past? Shall I be in the future? Shall I not be in the future? What shall I be in the future? Having been what, what shall I become in the future?" Or else he is inwardly perplexed about the present thus: "Am I? Am I not? What am I? How am I? Where has this being come from? Where will it go?"[3]

A complementary list of unanswered questions is found in the "Culamalunkya Sutta," or "Shorter Instructions to Malunka," where we read:

> These speculative views have been left undeclared by the Blessed One, set aside and rejected by him, namely: "the world is eternal" and "the world is not eternal;" "the world is finite" and "the world is not finite;" "the soul is the same as the body;" and "the soul is one thing and the body another;" and "after death a Tathagata exists" and "after death a Tathagat does not exist" and "after death a Tathagata both exists and does not exist" and "after death a Tathagata neither exists nor does not exist."[4]

If we understand these lists of unanswered questions as Pyrrhonian dilemmas, we can appreciate that what the Buddha means is that we should not "attend," as he puts it, to any such speculations, or beliefs, or interpretations, because they are "unfit for attention," because they lead us to ignorance and away from truth, away from dependent origination. Like the Pyrrhonists, the Buddha simply suspends judgment about them.

Dependent origination doesn't stop because one holds a belief; but the believer thinks it does, and to that extent loses consciousness of dependent origination, and becomes ignorant. The believer, the positive (or negative) dogmatist, who attends to speculation, becomes detached from the phenomenal reality organized as *pragmata*, and takes refuge instead in one or another imagined belief about what our *pragmata* mean. In the case of the negative dogmatist, he or she takes refuge in the nihilistic denial that *pragmata* can mean anything at all.

Speculation over dogmatic issues, avoided by the Buddha, can be understood as a psychological fixation, or neurosis, as in classical psychiatry and psychoanalysis. A neurosis (or psychosis) is an instance of compulsive-obsessive behavior, something repeated over and over again in an effort to assert its independent existence. The neurotic, or believer, does not accommodate experience, but is tragically bound to some belief which takes him or her out of the flow of experience and traps them in an endless, repetitive cycle in which time is frozen. Such attachment, which marks all true beliefs, is the cause of unnecessary suffering, from which liberation is nonetheless possible.

The Second Turning reveals the emptiness of all things as they actually are as the release from, and cure to, our neurosis. The vehicle of this revelation, in Pyrrhonian terms, is the judgment of the trilemma, that, for any belief, subject to an opposing belief in a dilemma, it is neither the case that the belief is true, nor that it is false. This is the suspension of judgment in the face of any dilemma, of any opposition in which it is said both that "X is Y" and that "X is not Y." It is the Buddha's refusal to engage in dilemma which opens the Middle Path to liberation.

Pyrrhonism clarifies the mechanism—elusive in the Buddhist literature—by which beliefs are established and the natural flow of experience is dammed up and frozen into a series of independently existing essences. Sextus, as we've seen, challenged the "indicative signs" employed by dogmatists (believers) to stand for things naturally non-evident. The indicative sign is a fictional interpretation of something we imagine presented *as if* it were real, and we are invited to presume it to be real. I can easily conjure up a mental picture or narrative of myself, for instance, as someone with a certain physical body—the guy I see in the mirror every morning—born at a certain time, with a history of experiences and behaviors, etc. It is when I interpret this mental picture or narrative as an indicative sign representing the real me—my actual self or identity, independently existing as the subject of the sum of my experiences and behaviors—that I create a belief in something non-evident, and, at the same time, invite its negation.

The creation and overcoming of a belief in an independently existing self—a belief which seems to be a container for all other beliefs—is the central issue of the First Turning. The creation of such a self is the major cause of personal suffering, we are told, and its dissolution the occasion of liberation. In the Second Turning we see that the imaginative projection of beliefs includes not only the projection of a self, but also the projection of an endless series of fictional essences which freeze the flow of experience, and fix the world in a series of rigid boxes. The self may be the ultimate container we imagine to include all these other essences, but the projection of their independent existence (to somewhere non-evident to us) has the effect of establishing an artificial dualism between the self and the world, subject and object. If the First Turning is the collapse of the self, the Second Turning is the collapse of the world. Both dissolve into the stream of consciousness, finally leaving no trace or karmic residue at all.

The Pyrrhonian equivalent of emptiness is absence, the opposite of presence. What is absent, or empty, is what is non-evident. In chapter three, we saw Sextus carefully distinguish between clear or evident facts, which are immediately present to us, and unclear or non-evident facts, the latter falling into three groups: those that are temporarily ("for the moment") non-evident, those that are absolutely ("naturally") non-evident, and those that are naturally ("once and for all") non-evident. It is worth rehearsing these Pyrrhonian distinctions once more, with an eye towards the Second Turning, or emptiness.

Temporarily non-evident facts are sensible facts which come and go more or less reliably, but which, when absent, can be re-presented to us by mental facts we find in memory and imagination. These enable us not only to navigate the ordinary world in normal life, but to better predict the future. Judgments of facts temporarily non-evident have the advantage that they can be tested, and confirmed or disconfirmed. Absolutely or naturally non-evident facts, by contrast, are absent facts which remain beyond our reach, and cannot be confirmed, or disconfirmed. Sextus' stock example is the absent fact of whether the number of stars is odd or even in number. We can see that stars exist, but also see that we have no way of determining their number because we lack any definite way of counting them.

The remaining group of non-evident facts—those Sextus calls naturally or "once and for all" non-evident—are not so easily explained, and are the most important for our purposes. These are "facts" imagined by dogmatists to be represented by "indicative" signs. There is nothing about dependent origination *per se* which precludes the possibility that such facts may exist somewhere outside of dependent origination as we know it, nor that what occurs in experience is solely dependently originated and not some kind of manifestation of naturally non-evident facts. Why, the dogmatist asks, shouldn't the forms displayed in *pragmata* represent substances or essences or externally existing independent realities of some kind? It's true that dependent origination won't allow us to correlate such essences with the forms actually displayed in *pragmata*, but why can't those essences be believed to somehow generate (or reflect) such forms from somewhere below, behind, beyond, or otherwise outside our *pragmata*?

In the Pyrrhonist understanding, consistent with what we know of Buddhism, naturally non-evident facts (e.g., the Self or Soul, or God, or Nature, etc.) can be redeemed, or realized, only in sensation. Only then is their emptiness, or absence, canceled out by their presence. Suppose Santa Claus was discovered by explorers to really live at the North Pole with Ms. Santa Claus, to have an actual workshop with actual Elves, an actual sleigh with actual reindeer, and so on. Santa would then become "real," as we would ordinarily say, a fact of experience, and no longer an "empty" notion. Similarly, the Self might someday be discovered located in the brain, perhaps, or God might actually appear in the heavens, peering down on us, as in the famous scene in the film *Monty Python and the Holy Grail*.[5]

Such discoveries would show that we were mistaken about what we took to be naturally or "once and for all" non-evident things since, in fact, they turned out to be not naturally but only temporarily non-evident. Their appearance in the transient sensory world of dependent origination would not, however, be the realization of a permanently existing independent entity or essence; it would only be a form, like any other, dependently displayed in the *pragmata* we experience. The emptiness of phenomena is the absence of any evidence of their independent existence. I might have the name of a student listed on the class printout for my course who fails to appear. Unlike the student who initially appears, and then fails to appear on subsequent occasions, this student never appears at all. The name of the student who never appears is naturally "empty," an "indicative" sign unrealized in flesh-and-blood. But the name is not nothing; it retains its own phenomenal existence as an item on the class printout.

Dependent origination admits of no mechanism by which essences can be established. Insofar as things dependently originated are necessarily empty, any kind of essence turns out to be necessarily absent. Things are either present or absent, realized (as *pragmata*) or empty. But whatever is realized (in thought and sensation) is no more (or less) than a dependently originated transient appearance of phenomena organized as a sensible fact, a sensible *pragma*. It has no basis in anything else; it has no independent existence.

The foremost Buddhist philosopher of the Second Turning, Nāgārjuna, writing in the second century CE, seamlessly merges dependent origination with emptiness. In his words:

Whatever is dependently co-arisen
That is explained to be emptiness.
That, being a dependent designation,
Is itself the middle way.
Something that is not dependently arisen,
Such a thing does not exist.
Therefore a non-empty thing
Does not exist.[6]

Even emptiness, Nāgārjuna tells us, is empty—hence the emptiness of emptiness, or the absence of absence.[7] The essence of emptiness, or absence, would be the real independent, if negative, existence of emptiness. Nāgārjuna's identification of dependent origination with emptiness undercuts the radical scepticism of the annihilationists, or Academic philosophers. The emptiness, or absence, to which negative dogmatists seek to reduce all things turns out—just like any positive dogmatism—to have no substance, no essence, nothing that can be realized, even negatively. Negative beliefs, like positive beliefs, can no more be refuted than confirmed. All our beliefs remain speculations or interpretations imposed upon our *pragmata*, as well as upon their absence, arising out of our ignorance of dependent origination.

The realization in consciousness of dependent origination comes across as a kaleidoscope of changing displays of forms which exist only as varying combinations of the universal recurring phenomena which make up our *pragmata*. Phenomena are the pixels, as it were, which light up the forms we perceive on the screen of consciousness. The more closely they are scrutinized, the more elusive they become, until, below a certain threshold, they simply disappear. Yet, at the same time, it is the consistent and predictable recurrence of many combinations of phenomena which brings reliability into the transient world.

Nāgārjuna has more to say. Emptiness, for him, is revealed through an eight-fold negation found in The Dedicatory Verses at the beginning of the *Mūlamadhyamakakārikā*, where he gives a summary of dependent origination, which, he tells us, is "neither extinct nor arising; neither having end nor eternal; neither one nor many; neither coming nor going."[8] Dependent origination turns out to be empty of all of these. The eight-fold negation is a series of dualisms. "One" and "many" are plain enough; "arising" can be understood as "existence," "extinct" as "non-existence," "end" as "finite," "eternal" as "infinite," "coming" and "going" as "presence" and "absence." If we do that, the eight-fold negation becomes a series of four dualisms:

Existence and Non-Existence
The Finite and the Infinite
The One and the Many
Presence and Absence.

Each pair presents us with a dilemma. It's either one or the other in each case—or so we are invited to think. Nāgārjuna's movement here is from dilemma to trilemma, trumping the former in favor of the latter. Instead of endlessly oscillating between one or the other of any dilemmic pair in fruitless debate, he points out that neither has to be the case, that the choice is not between one or the other, but includes a third option: that neither the one nor the other has to be accepted. And this option is at the same time a recognition of emptiness. Dependent origination is empty of both existence and non-existence, of both the finite and the infinite, of both the one and the many, and of both presence and absence.

To recognize the emptiness of polarizing absolutes like these is to recognize, to use Pyrrhonian language, that they are judgments to be suspended—whether affirmations or denials—and not facts to be believed. As Sextus puts it: "For anyone who holds beliefs on even one subject, or in general prefers one appearance to another in point of convincingness or lack of convincingness, or makes assertions about any unclear matter, thereby has the distinctive character of a Dogmatist."[9] Notice that a belief "on even one subject" is enough to fall into dogmatism.

While the list of beliefs recognized in Buddhist texts is fairly brief—like Nagarjuna's eight-negations, or the Buddha's own handful of "unanswered questions"—what we see by contrast in the Pyrrhonian

Emptiness and the suspension of belief 101

mirror of Buddhism is a rich and virtually endless series of beliefs, whether in ethics, logic, physics, mathematics, grammar, rhetoric, even poetry and art. Indeed, these are systematically examined head on in exhaustive detail by Sextus in his works, especially those other than the *Outlines of Scepticism*. These beliefs, on almost any subject, are all judgments about non-evident things, pro or con. As stated earlier, beliefs are things imagined which are presumed to exist (or not exist) somewhere outside our minds as real, permanent entities, even though there is no evidence of their actually being phenomenally realized. We can confirm some non-evident facts—those that are temporarily non-evident. And there are also facts—those absolutely non-evident—which we see cannot be determined. But the remaining facts—those naturally non-evident—can neither be confirmed nor dis-confirmed. The dogmatist can only insist on his or her belief in such facts, in the absence of confirmation. The Pyrrhonian Buddhist suspends judgment in recognition of the emptiness of such beliefs. The things left over the Pyrrhonists call "clear" or "evident'—the actual *pragmata* we experience as they come and go in our thoughts and sensations, in the phenomenal flow of dependent origination.

Notes

1 See Leonard C. D. C. Priestley, *Pudgalavāda Buddhism: The Reality of the Indeterminate Self* (Toronto: University of Toronto, Centre for South Asian Studies, South Asian Studies Papers No. 12, Monograph No. 1, 1999).
2 *Heart of Wisdom Sūtra*, http://www.bodhicitta.net/Heart%20of%20Wisdom%20Sutra.htm.
3 "Sabbāsava Sutta" in *The Middle Length Discourses of the Buddha (Majjhima Nikāya)*, trans. Bhikkhu Nanamoli and Bhikkhu Bodhi (Somerville, MA: Wisdom Press, 1995), 92.
4 Ibid., 533; see also the "Aggivacchagotta Sutta," op. cit., 590–4.
5 The God scene in *Monty Python and the Holy Grail* can be found in https://www.youtube.com/watch?v=Bj4ax1BRPqo.
6 Nāgārjuna, *The Fundamental Wisdom of the Middle Way* [*Mūlamadhyamakaāarikā*], trans. Jay L. Garfield (New York: Oxford University Press, 1995), chapter XXIV, section 18–19, 69.
7 Cf. C. W. Huntington, Jr. (with Geshe Wangchen), *The Emptiness of Emptiness: An Introduction to Early Indian Madhyamaka* (Honolulu: University of Hawaii Press, 1989).
8 Quoted by Gadjin M. Nagao in "Buddhist Ontology" in *Mādhyamaka and Yogācāra*, ed. Gadjin Nagao, trans. L. S. Kamamura (Albany: SUNY Press, 1991), 174; cf. Nāgārjuna, op. cit., 2.
9 Empiricus, *Outlines of Scepticism*, op. cit. vol. I, 58, 223.

7 *Ataraxia* and *Bodhi*

The Third Turning is almost impossible to write about. It is enlightenment itself—*bodhi* or *ataraxia*—something usually held to be beyond language. How could it possibly be the subject of this or any chapter anywhere? For anyone looking for a description of enlightenment, this objection is well taken. But enlightenment is a state of being, not a description of anything. It includes both the evident *and* the non-evident, although only the former can be described. Insofar as it is an understanding of experience, it is an existential not a descriptive understanding. The closest we can get in descriptive terms is the ontology of dependent origination—of the evident contrasted with the non-evident.

As a state of being, enlightenment is not a theory, or an interpretation, of anything. It is curious that in the Pali scriptures and other normative Buddhist accounts, enlightenment was frequently attained, sometimes by large groups all at once, typically after hearing a discourse by the Buddha, or one of his main disciples. Over time, it became a rarer, more difficult attainment. Today few if any would claim (or be credited with) the kind of comprehensive global enlightenment commonly conceded to the Buddha, and to many of his disciples—numbers likely exaggerated in the later Buddhist tradition, in which he gained virtually divine status.

The Pyrrhonian tradition, if understood to reflect early, not normative, Buddhism, reflects a different approach to enlightenment—which it calls tranquility or *ataraxia*. If *nirvana* is the release which comes with suspension of judgment, *bodhi* is the tranquility, or *ataraxia*, which follows release. The impression given by the Pyrrhonian texts, especially those of Sextus Empiricus, is not that of a culminating, rather sudden enlightenment, but rather that of a series of mini-enlightenments, in which one is delivered from the bondage of one belief after another, in an ongoing sequence. This does not, however, necessarily preclude a cumulative or globalizing effect. In the normative Buddhist tradition, the Buddha's enlightenment came to be concentrated, perhaps mythically, into a single event, the culmination of his long night of meditation under the bodhi tree in Bodhgaya.

It would seem that the consistent ability of the Pyrrhonists to detect and defuse the beliefs they encountered implies a capacity to recognize *any* belief as a belief, and thereby to achieve some kind of liberation from *all* beliefs. The emergence of this ability—the recognition of its general applicability—suggests something like a moment of global conscious realization, perhaps not so different from what the Buddha is reported to have experienced under the bodhi tree.

Diogenes' life of Pyrrho implies that something similar may have happened to Pyrrho, most likely on the occasion of his encounter with the *gymnosophists* in India. That was the moment, as Diogenes reports, when Pyrrho was led to adopt his "most noble philosophy," featuring suspension of judgment and tranquility. Like the Buddha after Bodhgaya, Pyrrho after the *gymnosophists* realized and maintained a remarkable consistency, or peace of mind. No further philosophical development was noted, or necessary, it seems, for either Pyrrho or the Buddha.

In the Third Turning—represented most fully by the Yogācāra tradition—the experience of enlightenment emerges out of the conditions set by dependent origination (the First Turning) and emptiness (the Second Turning). There is no reason not to think of the First and Second Turnings as complementary, and even reversible: dependent origination requires emptiness, after all, as much as emptiness requires dependent origination. They come together, like two sides of a coin. Dependent origination without emptiness would be presence without absence; emptiness without dependent origination would be absence without presence. To insist on presence without absence would be a positive dogmatic belief, an assertion of some kind of permanent existence; to insist on absence without presence would be a negative dogmatic belief, an assertion that nothing can exist at all, or nihilism. Here again we encounter the two extremes between which the Buddha threaded the Middle Path.

The Pyrrhonists appear to have started with emptiness; they feature it prominently as suspension of judgment, the immediate goal of their practice, and proceed from there to their version of dependent origination, which, as argued in this book, they understood as phenomenalistic atomism The early Buddhists, by contrast, seem to have started with dependent origination, or phenomenalistic atomism of, as set out by the Buddha's first sermon, and proceeded from there to emptiness.

The Pyrrhonian focus on suspension of judgment as the most prominent step in their therapy (activated by the equipollence of opposing arguments, as catalogued in the modes) may reflect an initial breakthrough experience of emptiness, as perhaps occurred to Pyrrho in his contacts with Indian *gymnosophists*. That could have prompted him to transform the speculative atomism of Democritus he had brought with him into a phenomenal atomism that makes sense of what's left over when beliefs cancel out one another, and are suspended. And, to follow the path in the opposite direction, the original Buddhist focus on dependent origination would have implied suspension of judgment with regard to beliefs (the "unanswerable questions"), leading to the realization of emptiness.

Either way, we arrive at the Third Turning, expressed by the quadrilemma: that it is the case *both* that "X is Y," *and* that "X is not-Y." In "X is Y," X is an evident fact which can be demonstrated to signify another evident fact, Y, which turns out to be temporarily non-evident. In "X is not-Y," X is an evident fact which cannot be demonstrated to signify another evident fact, Y, which Sextus understood, in his language, to be "naturally" non-evident. The quadrilemma clarifies what is present and what it is not, what can be actually signified (using "commemorative" signs) and what cannot be signified (using "indicative" signs).

In other words, it is just as true to say that our beliefs are both true and false (the Third Turning, or quadrilemma) as it is true to say that they are neither true nor false (the Second Turning, or trilemma). In the case of the quadrilemma, in which *both* "X = Y" and "X = not Y" are affirmed, we recognize that X and Y are both phenomenally realized, but that Y appears phenomenally only in thought, not in sensation, while X appears in both. In the quadrilemma, we recognize the empty reality of belief as evident in the lack of correlation with any phenomena the belief is said to represent.

In response to the Second Turning, or trilemma, which says No to saying either Yes or No to something, and which thereby recognizes its emptiness, we proceed, in the Third Turning, or quadrilemma, to say Yes to saying either Yes or No to something. In Pyrrhonian terms we accept both the assertion of a belief, *and* its denial. While beliefs (dogmatic assertions, pro and con) are denied in the Second Turning, in the Third Turning, or quadrilemma, they are recognized for what they are, namely, beliefs, or purported signs that cannot be shown to signify what they are believed to signify. Thus exposed, they are neutralized and folded back into the flux of impermanent phenomena, which can finally be recognized for the flow of dependent

Ataraxia *and* Bodhi 105

origination that it is; we no longer need to suffer in ignorance because of our beliefs.

What it means to believe in something is to presume that something we can only imagine exists somewhere independently of us, out of our imagination, and could somehow be realized for us in reality, in sensation. The grownups know, for instance, that the man impersonating Santa Claus at the shopping center or town square during the holidays is not "really" Santa Claus. They recognize that he represents no more than a sign or token of an idea of Santa Claus; nonetheless, the child accompanying the grownups is encouraged to believe otherwise, to continue, in ignorance, to think that this man really is Santa Claus. A "real" Santa Claus, after all, would have to appear in sensation, in the physical world, independently of our thoughts, just as the impersonator does, and not just be a function or projection of our imagination of him.

The Yogācāra not only recognized but made central the role of the imagination in producing belief, and thereby ignorance, the price of belief. They located the realization of enlightenment as a state of being following upon what the *Saṃdhinirmocana*—the sūtra in which the Three Turnings are first introduced—calls the recognition of the Three Natures, or Three Worlds. In Chapter 6, "The Questions of Gunakara," the Buddha proclaims: "Gunakara, there are three characteristics of phenomena ... They are the imputational character, the other-dependent character, and the thoroughly established character."[1]

The "imputational" nature is what is imagined to exist, the "other-dependent" nature is what is dependently originated, and the "thoroughly established character" is what is consummated or thoroughly perfected, or *bodhi* itself. The imagined nature is comprised of the fictional facts we construct in thought—of everything we can imagine but which does not exist (or can't be found) in sensation. Insofar as we imagine that our fictional creations signify non-fictional facts, they are beliefs, just as the Pyrrhonists insisted. The imagined nature of Yogācāra corresponds to the world of beliefs made plain by the Pyrrhonians, just as the dependently originated nature of the Yogācāra corresponds to the Pyrrhonian world of intermittent phenomenal *pragmata*, as we've seen earlier.

The Yogācāra, like all Buddhists, adopt the dependent origination of the First Turning, as propounded in the early texts, just as the Pyrrhonists do by way of their phenomenalistic atomism. The Yogācāra also adopt the emptiness of the Second Turning, expressed by the Pyrrhonists as absence, or the evidently non-evident. The Yogācāra, in the Third Turning, takes the further step of demonstrating that our beliefs, or fictional creations, are confined to the imagination, insofar as they cannot be found in the world of sensation. The belief that a mental event represents an independently existing event presumes that anything we can imagine can be realized (somewhere, somehow, someday) in sensation. By the same token, the abandonment of that belief clarifies the dependent origination of thoughts and sensations. This sense of final clarity is what the "The Questions of Paramarthasamudgata" in the *Saṃdhinirmocana* seems to be offering when it speaks of the Third Turning as no less than "the teaching of the ultimate, the definite meaning."[2]

The effect of any belief is to obscure dependent origination—the changing phenomenal forms displayed in *pragmata*—in favor of an *idee fixe* which locks down the flow of experience. An imagined fiction asserts itself insofar as it becomes a standard by which the flow of experience is defined, anticipated, captured, and frozen. If I believe in Santa Claus, for instance, I anticipate his yearly Christmas visit, and act accordingly. I hang stockings to receive his presents and listen for his sleigh on my roof. When I open my stocking on Christmas morning and find it full of presents, I take it as confirmation of his visit. Much of what Christmas Eve and Christmas Day mean are informed by such imaginative projections, or beliefs, which powerfully interpret the sensations we actually experience. Beliefs in this way become the criteria of behavior, of ritual, of reality itself.

The same is true of the more serious parts of Christmas. A Christian believer imagines the birth of Jesus in a manger in Bethlehem, as well as the larger story of the prophecies of a coming messiah, of Caesar's edict of taxation, of "no room at the inn," of the manger and the shepherds, of the wise men, of the flight into Egypt, etc. For the believer, some kind of reenactment of this story is the essential content of the holiday. Believers behave in real life as if the story actually happened; they re-react it in ritual. The more the fiction, the story, is used to interpret and thereby structure our experience, the more inflexible and permanent it becomes, and the fewer are the deviations from it which can be tolerated. Its use as a standard of behavior establishes a drive towards uniformity, and ultimately censorship and control. Competing versions of imaginative projection raise doubts and undermine the efficacy of the ritualized process of acting out the belief, and cannot be convincingly adjudicated. To successfully impose a fiction as a standard of experience, as an instrument of our will, it must be clear and distinct, ultimately intolerant of competitors.

It is this imagined nature of mental fictions which allows us to posit a world outside of dependent origination, outside of *pragmata* as we know them. Experience is externalized and fixed by virtue of our beliefs about the world—pictures in our minds—which take on the character of seemingly independently existing objects. The flow of events manifest in dependent origination is masked by these beliefs, which instead provide interpretations of those events. The objectification of beliefs (granting them an independent existence) invites a corresponding subjectivization of our thoughts and sensations (which end up inside of us). The result is a dichotomized world of inside and outside, subject and object.

Most of us live in a world of beliefs. They can be as mundane as a belief in Santa Claus, or as serious as a belief in the divinity of Jesus, the dictatorship of the proletariat, the "hidden hand" of capitalism, the "master race," "American exceptionalism," and many, many more, including interpretations of truth, justice, love, art, and so on. The systematic deconstruction of virtually any belief—evident throughout Sextus' works—points to the uncompromising philosophical radicalism shared by Pyrrhonists and early Buddhists alike. *Ataraxia* and *bodhi* require that we lead a life without beliefs.

Vasubandhu, writing later on the Three Natures, clearly identifies the imagination as the mechanism for the construction of belief; he shows that recognizing the dependent nature of what we imagine is the clue to realizing that beliefs are fictions, not independently existing realities. That, he maintains, is the precondition for liberation (*nirvana*), leading to enlightenment (*bodhi, ataraxia*). When we imagine something as having an independent existence we imagine it as existing apart from us, just as we imagine what we see on a motion picture screen as existing apart from us in its own separate reality, even though we know better.

Vasubandhu, developing the insights of the *Saṃdhinirmocana*, famously uses a simile suggested there, of a magic show, in Verses 27 and 28 in his *Treatise of the Three Natures* to make this point:

> Like an elephant that appears
> Through the power of a Magician's mantra—
> Only the precept appears,
> The elephant is completely non-existent
>
> The imagined nature is the elephant;
> The other-dependent nature if the visual percept;
> The non-existence of the elephant therein
> Is explained to be the consummate.[3]

In the magic show, the magician holds up an image—a picture, perhaps painted on a piece of wood, or perhaps a mask or silhouette—and, by invocation (the all-important mantra, the affirmative act of will), he proclaims the independent existence of an actual elephant. Look! There it is! We are invited to a willing suspension of disbelief. The key step here—the mantra—is not only an invitation to belief, but a performative act which enables, and makes possible, that belief. We are invited to suspend what should be the normal judgment of dependent origination—in which the image of the elephant remains no more than an image. In its place, we are asked to project *through that image* the existence of an actual external reality, of a "real" elephant, which exists in a different world from the one in which we are sitting, in an audience, watching the magician. We are invited, in our minds, to leave the darkened theater, to forget the magician, and cross over into a separate, imagined world in which we pretend that we experience the real existence of an elephant. We not only join into the story or narrative that is offered, we identify with it through a willing suspension of disbelief.

The objectification of the elephant into an independently existing thing is at the same time the subjectification of the audience and magician in the theater. The audience and the magician do not disappear, but they are marginalized, while attention is drawn instead to what we are being asked to imagine as real. A kind of trance-like state is invoked. We ignore that we are sitting in an audience, and go off into a projected mental space where we entertain a collective hallucination—where we "see" an elephant and accept its reality. Paradoxically, the real world of dependently originated thoughts and sensations (the forms actually displayed by *pragmata*) is made illusory, while an illusory world of imagined belief is made real. This inversion of reality is the hallmark of belief.

Liberation, or *nirvana*, is the undoing of this inversion; it is the restoration of dependent origination, of seeing things as they really are, as the Buddha repeatedly puts it, leading to the peace of *bodhi*, or *ataraxia*. If anyone should ask for a formula for achieving *bodhi*, one might reply: subtract the "imputational nature," or what is imagined, from the "other-dependent" nature, and you will be left with the consummated, or "thoroughly perfect" nature of enlightenment, or *bodhi*. In Pyrrhonian terms, subtract your beliefs from what you actually experience of phenomenalistic atomism, and you will arrive at *pragmata* as they really are.

Once we make the distinction between external and internal, between what we believe to be the case and what is actually the case, we have no choice but to distinguish between what is not us (what is outside of us) and what is us (what is inside of us). The illusion of belief entails not just the illusion of self, but the illusion of other. The disillusion of belief is the disillusion of both self and other and their merger in the rebirth of non-duality. For the Yogācāra, like the Pyrrhonists, there is no independently existing reality, no dichotomy of objective and subjective, external and internal, and no distinction between them.

The disillusion of self and other leaves us, according to the Yogācāra as well as the Pyrrhonists, with the objects of which we are actually or directly conscious, or what the Yogācāra call "consciousness only." These are not the independently existing objects of the believer, which remain out of reach, but rather the dependently existing objects present to consciousness, that is, our phenomena as organized into *pragmata*. Beyond them there is only absence, or the non-evident.

The suspension of belief in fictional imaginings, integral to Pyrrhonian Buddhism, returns us to the flux of dependent origination, that is, to *pragmata* as interdependent combinations of phenomena displaying forms. That forms are dependently realized can be recognized only if we abandon the impulse to belief, and its beguiling claim that certain things we imagine have a permanent, independent existence which is determinative of what we perceive.

The Yogācāra makes it clear that folding our imaginative projections, our beliefs, back into dependent origination reveals them for what they are, and dissolves the dichotomy of subject and object, self and other. The disappearance of belief is the condition for the disappearance of the independently existing objects, including an independently existing self, which only belief can sustain. Only the dependent phenomena of experience survive the disappearance of belief, insofar as they are displayed in the *pragmata* manifest in thought and sensation; they are neither subject nor object, internal nor external. Instead, they stand in consciousness as the phenomena with which we are immediately and directly acquainted—a state not to be confused with subjective idealism. This is not some "inner state," but simply the unmediated consciousness of phenomena in their mutual dependency into which we dissolve.

As least one Buddhist scholar, Thomas A. Kochumuttom, draws similar conclusions about Yogācāra:

> ... it must be noted that this is the whole point and central argument of the Yogācāra philosophy: the entire lot of *saṃsāra*

experience hinges on the polar concepts of subjectivity and objectivity (*grāhakatva* and *grāhyatva*) namely that one is the subject of experience (*bhoktṛ*), while all else are objects of one's experience (*bhojya*); then the concept of objectivity is proved to be mere imagination, which will in turn prove the concept of subjectivity as well to be mere imagination; thus the concepts of subjectivity and objectivity collapsing, the whole *saṃsāra* experience, too, collapses, and there automatically results release (*mokṣa* or *mukti* or *nirvāṇa*).[4]

The impulse to belief can be abandoned only if we understand the mechanism of belief as an imaginative projection, if we see it for what it is, not for what we believe it to be. Belief is the affirmation (or negation) of that mechanism—the insistence that it represents (or fails to represent) a reality beyond itself. To be free of it is to recognize its emptiness. The imagination, it turns out, is as dependently originated as anything else. *Bodhi*, or *ataraxia*, arises out of the suspension of belief, out of *nirvana*, out of the Pyrrhonian-Buddhist recognition of what remains after the world of the imagination collapses back into the world of *pragmata*, or dependent origination.

Dependent origination is not only about phenomena which are present in consciousness; it is also about those which are absent. If the self is the absence which accompanies all things present, then there is indeed no self as we might imagine it, as the Buddha proclaimed. But this is not to say that the self is absolutely nothing at all. It is merely an absence evident in this world, something which is not present, but which might yet be, something perhaps possible, but in the meantime wholly indeterminate.

Notes

1 *Wisdom of Buddha: The Saṃdhinirmocana Sūtra*, trans. John Powers (Berkeley, CA: Dharma Publishing, 1995), 81.
2 Ibid., 145.
3 Vasubandhu, *Treatise on the Three Natures* [*Trisvabhāvanirdeśa*], trans. Jay L. Garfield, https://info-buddhism.com/Vasubandhu-Three_Natures-Garfield.html.
4 Thomas A. Kochumuttom, *A Buddist Doctrine of Experience: A New Translation and Interpretation of the Works of Vasubandhu the Yogācārin* (Delhi: Motilal Banarsidass, 1989), 11.

Bibliography

"Abidharma." *Stanford Encyclopedia of Philosophy*, https://plato.stanford.edu/entries/abhidharma/.
"Agamas." *The Encyclopedia of Buddhism*, https://encyclopediaofbuddhism.org/wiki/Agamas.
"Aggivacchagotta Sutta." The Middle Length Discourses of the Buddha (Majjhima Nikaya). Translated by Bhikkhi Nanamoli and Bhikkhu Bodhi. Somerville: Wisdom Press, 1995.
Anderson, Tenshin Reb. "Why the Wheel Turns Three Times." *Lion's Roar*, May 14, 2012. https://www.lionsroar.com/why-the-wheel-turns-three-times/.
Annas, Julia. "Ancient Scepticism and Ancient Religion." *Episteme, etc: Essays in Honor of Jonathan Barnes*, edited by Ben Morison and Katerina Lerodiakonou, 74–89. Oxford: Oxford University Press, 2011.
Beckwith, Christopher. "Early Buddhism and Incommensurability." *Philosophy East and West 68*, no. 2 (July 2018), 1009–1016.
Beckwith, Christopher I. *Greek Buddha: Pyrrho's Encounter with Early Buddhism in Central Asia*, Princeton, NJ: Princeton University Press, 2015.
Berkeley, George. *Principles, Dialogues, and Philosophical Correspondence*, edited by Colin Murray Turbayne. Indianapolis: Bobbs-Merrill Company, Library of Liberal Arts, 1965.
Berryman, Sylvia. "Democritus" *Stanford Encyclopedia of Philosophy*. Revised December 2, 2016, https://plato.stanford.edu.entries/democritus/.
Bett, Richard. *Pyrrho: His Antecedents and His Legacy*. Oxford: Oxford University Press, 2000.
Blumenthal, James. *"Three Turnings of the Wheel of Dharma," Mandala*, October/December 2008.
Bodhi, Bhikkhu. "Introduction." *The Middle Length Discourses of the Buddha: A Translation of the Majjhima Nikaya*. Translated by Bhikkhu Nanamoli and Bhikkhu Bodhi. Boston, MA: Wisdom Publications, 2005.
Brons, Robin. "Life without Belief: A Madhyamaka Defense of the Livability of Pyrrhonism." *Philosophy East and West 68*, no. 2 (April 2018), 329–351.

Buddhism and Scepticism: Historical, Philosophical, and Comparative Perspectives, edited by O. Hanner. Hamburg Buddhist Studies 12. Bochum/Freiburg: ProjektVerlag, 2020.

Clayman, Dee L. *Timon of Phlius: Pyrrhonism into Poetry.* Berlin: De Gruyter, 2009.

Collingwood, R. G. *The Idea of History,* edited by T. M. Knox. Eastford, CT: Martino Fine Books, 2014 [1946].

Conze, E. "Buddhist Philosophy and Its European Parallels." *Philosophy East and West 19:* 9–23.

Empiricus, Sextus. *Against the Ethicists.* Translated by Richard Bett Oxford: Oxford University Press, 1997.

Empiricus, Sextus. *Against the Logicians.* Translated by Richard Bett. Cambridge: Cambridge University Press, 2005.

Empiricus, Sextus. *Against the Physicists.* Translated by Richard Bett. Cambridge: Cambridge University Press, 2012.

Empiricus, Sextus. *Complete Works.* Translated by R. G. Bury, 4 vols. Cambridge: Harvard University Press, Loeb Classical Library, 1933–1949.

Empiricus, Sextus. *Outlines of Scepticism.* Translated by Julia Annas, and Jonathan Barnes. Cambridge: Cambridge University Press, 1994.

Garfield, Jay L. "Epoche and Sunyata: Skepticism East and West." *Philosophy East and West 40*, no. 3 (1990), 285–307.

Garfield, Jay L. "The Three Turnings of the Wheel of Dharma—Why They Are Essential to All of Us." Public Talk, Berlin, August 2011. https://info-buddhism.com/Three_Turnings_of_The_Wheel_of_Dharma_Jay_Garfield.html, https://info-buddhism.com/Three_Turnings_of_The_Wheel_of_Dharma_Jay_Garfield.html, https://info-buddhism.com/Three_Turnings_of_The_Wheel_of_Dharma_Jay_Garfield.html, https://info-buddhism.com/Three_Turnings_of_The_Wheel_of_Dharma_Jay_Garfield.html.

Gellius, Aulus. "Some Brief Notes about the Pyrrhonian Philosophers and the Academics; and of the Difference between Them." *Attic Nights II.* Translated by John C. Rolf, book XI, Chapter 5, 309–13. Cambridge, MA: Harvard University Press, Loeb Classical Library.

Gethin, Rupert. "He Who Sees Dhamma Sees Dhammas: Dhamma in Early Buddhism." *Journal of Indian Philosophy 32* (2004), 513–542.

Gethin, Rupert. *The Foundations of Buddhism*, Kindle Edition. Oxford: Oxford University Press, 2008, 44, quoted in "Agama" in *The Encyclopedia of Buddhism.* https://encyclopediaofbuddhism.org/wiki/Agamas.

Goodman, Charles. "Neither Scythian nor Greek: A Response to Beck with's Greek Buddha and Kuzminski's "Early Buddhism Reconsidered"." *Philosophy East and West 68*, no. 2 (July 2018), 984–1006.

Grgic, Fllip. "Sextus Empiricus on the Goal of Scepticism." *Ancient Philosophy 26* (2006), 141–60.

Halkias, Georgios. "The Self-Immolation of Kalanos and Other Luminous Encounters among Greeks and Indian Buddhists in the Hellenistic World." *Journal of the Oxford Centre for Buddhist Studies 8* (2015), 163–186.

Halkias, Georgios. *"When the Greeks Converted the Buddha: Asymmetrical Transfers of Knowledge in Indo-Greek Cultures."* Religions and Trade: Religious Formation, Transformation and Cross-Cultural Exchange Between East and West, edited by Peter Wick and Volker Rabens, 65–115. Leiden: Brill, 2014.

Hankinson, R. J. *The Sceptics.* London: Routledge, 1995.

Heart of Wisdom Sutra. http://www.bodhicitta.net/Heart%20of%20Wisdom%20Sutra.htm.

Hume, David. *An Inquiry Concerning Human Understanding*, 2nd ed. Indianapolis: Hackett Publishing Company, 1993.

Huntington, Jr., C.W. *The Emptiness of Emptiness: An Introduction to Early Indian Madhyamaka.* Honolulu: University of Hawaii Press, 1989.

Husserl, Edmund. *The Idea of Phenomenology.* Translated by William P. Alston and George Nakhnikian. The Hague: Martinus Nijhoff, 1964.

Inglis, Fred. *History Man: The Life of R. G. Collingwood.* Princeton, NJ: Princeton University Press, 2009.

Jackson, William J. "Self Immolation in Hindu, Buddhist, and Other Traditions." https://www.academia.edu/4866752/Self-Immolation_in_Hindu_Buddhist_and_Other_Traditions.

Johnson, Monte Ransome, and Shults, Brett. "Early Pyrrhonism as a Sect of Buddhism: A Case Study in the Methodology of Comparative Philosophy." *Comparative Philosophy 9*, no. 2 (2018), 1–40.

Kochumuttom, Thomas A. *A Buddhist Doctrine of Experience: A New Translation of the Works of Vasubandhu the Yogacara.* Delhi: Motilal Banarsidass Publishers, 1989.

Kuzminski, Adrian. *Pyrrhonism: How the Ancient Greeks Reinvented Buddhism.* Lanham, MD: Lexington Books, 2008.

Kuzminski, Adrian. "Early Buddhism Reconsidered." *Philosophy East and West 68*, no. 2, (July 2018), 974–983.

Kuzminski, Adrian. Reply to Charles Goodman. *Philosophy East and West 68*, no. 2 (July 2018), 1007–1009.

Laertius, Diogenes. *Lives of Eminent Philosophers.* 2 vols. Translated by R. D. Hicks. Cambridge: Harvard University Press, Loeb Classical Library, 1925.

Laertius, Diogenes. *Lives of Eminent Philosophers.* Translated by Pamela Mensch. Oxford: Oxford University Press, 2018.

Long, A. A., and D. N. Sedley. *The Hellenistic Philosophers*, vol 1, Translations of the Principal Sources with Philosophical Commentary. Cambridge: Cambridge University Press, 1992.

Lusthaus, Dan. *Buddhist Phenomenology: A Philosophical Investigation of Yogacara Buddhism and the Ch'eng Wei-shin lun.* New York: Routledge Curzon, 2003.

Lusthaus, Dan. "The Heart Sutra in Chinese Yogacara: Some Comparative Comments on the Heart Sutra Commentaries of Wonch'uk and K'uei-chi." *International Journal of Buddhist Thought and Culture*, September 2003, vol 3. https://www.academia.edu/225330/The_Heart_S%C5%ABtra_in_Chinese_Yog%C4%81c%C4%81ra_Some_Comparative_Comments_on_the_Heart_S%C5%ABtra_Commentaries_of_W%C5%8Fnch%C5%ADk_and_Kuei-chi?email_work_card=view-paper.

Lusthaus, Dan. "What Is and Isn't Yogacara." *Yogacara Buddhism Research Association*. http://www.acmuller.net/yogacara/articles/intro.html.

Majjhima Nikaya. *The Middle Length Discourses of the Buddha: A Translation of the Majjhima Nikaya*. Translated by Bhikhu Nanamoli and Bhikku Bodhi, I, 190–1. Boston: Wisdom Publications, 3rd ed., 2005, 284.

Massie, Pascal. "Ataraxia: Tranquility at the End." In *A Companion to Ancient Philosophy*, edited by Sean D Kirkland and Eric Sanday, 245–262. Evanston: Northwestern University Press, 2018.

McEvilley, Thomas. *The Shape of Ancient Thought: Comparative Studies in Greek and Indian Philosophies*. New York: Allworth Press. 2001.

Monty Python and the Holy Grail. https://www.youtube.com/watch?v=Bj4ax1BRPqo.

Nagao, Gadjin M. "Buddhist Ontology." *Madhyamaka and Yogacara*, edited by Gadjin Nagao, translated by L. S. Kamamura. Albany: SUNY Press, 1991.

Nagarjuna. *The Fundamental Wisdom of the Middle Way [Mulamadhyamakakarika]*. Translated by Jay L. Garfield. New York: Oxford University Press, 1995.

Neale, Matthew. "*Madhyamaka and Pyrrhonism: Doctrinal, Linguistic, and Historical Parallels Between Madhyamaka Buddhism & Hellenic Pyrrhonism.*" DPhil. diss., Regent's Park College, University of Oxford, August, 2014.

Nietzsche, Friedrich. *The Will to Power*. Translated by Walter Kaufmann. New York: Vintage Books, 1968.

O'Keefe, Tim. "The Cyrenaics vs. the Pyrrhonists on Knowledge of Appearances." *New Essays on Ancient Pyrrhonism*, edited by Diego Machuca. Leiden: Brill, 2011.

Orsborn, Matt (Huifeng) B. "'Dependent Origination = Emptiness'—Nargajuna's Innovation? An Examination of the Early and Mainstream Sectarian Textual Sources." *Journal for the Centre of Buddhist Studies, Sri Lanka XI* (2013), 1–53.

Pausanias. *Guide to Greece*. 2 vols. Translated by Peter Levi. New York: Penguin Books, 1971.

The Perfection of Wisdom in Eight Thousand Lines & Its Verse Summary. Translated by Edward Conze. San Francisco, CA: City Lights, 1973.

Popkin, Richard. *The History of Scepticism from Erasmus to Spinoza*. Berkeley, CA: University of California Press, 1979.

Priestly, Leonard C. D. C. *Pudgalavada Buddhism: The Reality of the Indeterminate Self*. Toronto: University of Toronto Press, Centre for

Bibliography 115

South Asian Studies, South Asian Studies Papers No. 12, Monograph No. 1, 1999.
Pyrrhonian Skepticism in Diogenes Laertius: Introduction, Text, Translation, Commentary and Interpretative Essays, edited by Katja Maria Vogt. Essays by Katja Maria Vogt, Richard Bett, Lorenzo Corti, Tiziano Dorandi, Christiana M. M. Olfert, Elisabeth Scharffenberger, David Sedley, and James Warren. Tubingen: Mohr Siebeck, 2015.
Ray, Reginald. "What Is Dharma." *Lion's Roar: Buddhist Wisdom for our Time*, December 26, 2017. https://www.lionsroar.com/in-a-word-dharma/.
Reddoch, M. Jason. "Review of Pyrrhonism: How the Ancient Greeks Reinvented Buddhism." *Philosophy East and West 60*, no. 3 (July 2010), 424–427.
"Sabbasava Sutta." *The Middle Length Discourses of the Buddha (Majjhima Nikaya)*. Translated by Bhikkhu Nanamoli and Bhikkhu Bodhi. Somerville, MA: Wisdom Press, 1995.
"Samyuta Nikaya," V, 56, 11. *The Connected Discourses of the Buddha: A Translation of the Samyuta Nikaya*. Translated by Bhikkhu Bodhi, 1843–1847. Boston, MA: Wisdom Publications, 2000.
Shulman, Eviatar. *Rethinking the Buddha: Early Buddhist Philosophy as Meditative Perception*. Cambridge: Cambridge University Press, 2014.
Shults, Brett, and Ransome, Monte. "Early Pyrrhonism as a Sect of Buddhism: A Case Study in the Methodology of Comparative Philosopy." *Comparative Philosophy 9*, no. 2 (2018), 1–40.
Siderits, Mark. *Philosophy as Buddhism: An Introduction*. Indianapolis: Hackett Publishing, 2007.
Singer, P. N. "Galen" *The Stanford Encyclopedia of Philosophy*, March 18, 2016. https://plato.stanford.edu/entries/galen.
Smith, David Woodruff. "Phenomenology." *Stanford Encyclopedia of Philosophy* (revised December 16, 2013). https://plato.stanford.edu /entries/phemenology/.
Stcherbatsky, Theodore. *The Central Conception of Buddhism and the Meaning of the Word "Dharma."* Delhi: Motilal Banarsidass Publishers, 2018 [1922].
Stcherbatsky, Theodore. *The Conception of Buddhist Nirvana*. New York: Samuel Weiser, 1968.
Stoneman, Richard. *The Greek Experience of India: From Alexander to the Indo-Greeks*. Princeton, NJ: Princeton University Press, 2019.
"Sutta-Nipata." Translated by H. Saddhatissa. London: Curzon Press, 1985.
Urstadt, Kristian. "Review of Pyrrhonism: How the Ancient Greeks Reinvented Buddhism." *Journal of Buddhist Ethics 17* (2010): 56–65.
Vasubandhu. "Thirty Verses on Consciousness Only." Ben Connelly, *Inside Vasubandhu's Yogacara: A Practitioner's Guide*. Translated by Ben Connelly and Weijen Teng. Somerville, MA: Wisdom Publications, 2016.
Vasubandhu. *Trimsatika [Thirty Verses] of Vasubandhu*, translated by Anonymous. Wutai Mountain, 2008. https://wutai.wordpress.com/2008/02/13/trimsatika-thirty-verses-of-vasubandhu/.

Bibliography

Vasubandhu. *Trisvabhavanirdesa*. Translated by Jay L. Garfield. In Chapter VII, "Vasubandhu's Treatise on the Three Natures: A Translation and Commentary." In Jay L. Garfield, *Empty World: Buddhist Philosophy and Cross Cultural Interpretation*. Oxford: Oxford University Press, 2002. See also: https://info-buddhism.com/Vasubandhu-Three_Natures-Garfield.html.

Walters, Jonathan S. *Finding Buddhists in Global History*. Washington, DC: American Historical Association, 1998.

Wisdom of Buddha: The Samdhinimocana Sutra. Translated by John Powers. Berkeley, CA: Dharma Publishing, 1994.

Index

Abhidharma 78, 81, 110
Academics 36–7, 60, 62–3, 73
adiaphora 9
Aenesidemus 30–1, 46
Against the Learned (or *Professors*) (Sextus Empiricus) 36, 40–1
Against the Logicians (Sextus Empiricus) 43–4, 46
Agamas 2
Agrippa 30
Alexander the Great 2, 4–6, 22
anatman 9
Anaxarchus 4, 10, 13, 26, 55
Anderson, T.A. 68
anepikrita 9
anitya 9
Annihilationism/Annihilationists 65–6, 72–5, 84, 87, 89–90, 99
Antigonus Gonatas 53
Apollonius 24
Aporetics 26
appearances 42; phenomenological understanding of 56
Arcesilaus 37
arhat 94
Aristippus 10
Aristocles 52–3, 57
Aristocles passage 3, 8–9, 21, 57, 65
Aristototelians 35–6
assertion of judgment 59–60
astathmeta 9
ataraxia 3, 13, 26, 35–6, 48–9, 65, 102–10
athambia 13, 26
Athenaeus 53

atomism 14–15, 80, 104
Attic Nights (Gellius) 21, 60–3
Aulus Gellius 3, 21, 60–3

Beckwith, C. 4, 7–9
beliefs: abandonment of 48; negative 69, 99; positive 38, 69, 99
Bett, R. 11
Bhikkhu Bodhi 76
bhojya 110
bhoktṛ 110
Biudd 81
Blumenthal, J. 68
Bodhgaya 103
bodhi 3, 25, 35, 65, 69, 95, 102–10
bodhisattva 95
brahmanas 5
Bryson 10, 52
Buddha 2, 23, 65, 74–7, 86, 93, 105, 108; on dependent origination 74; on duality of dilemma 70; enlightenment 102–3; liberation 26; meditative states 49; Middle Path 71; *Sakyamuni* 7; sayings 66; sermons 67–70; unanswered questions 95–6, 100; on volitional formations 76; and Zoroastrianism 8–9
Buddhism 2; early 1, 7–8, 21, 36, 65–6, 77–8, 92, 105; normative 7–9, 72, 78, 83–4, 102; phenomenalistic atomism of 80–1; Pyrrhonian 3, 9, 14, 16, 59, 66, 78–80, 83, 86–9, 92, 94, 109; and Pyrrhonism 1–3
Buddhism as Philosophy (Siderits) 81

Index

Buddhist Phenomenalism
   (Lusthaus) 86
Buddhists 2–7, 9, 14, 16–18, 25–6, 28,
   33, 38–9, 44, 65–7, 71–2, 76–7, 81,
   87–9, 92–3, 103, 105
Burnet, J. 1

Callisthenes 4
Carneades 37
causation 80
Christmas 106
Clayman, D.L. 53–5
Cleobulus 4
Clitomachus 37
cogitatio 56
Collingwood, R.G. 17–8, 65
commemorative signs 47–8
Crates 12
Culamalunkya Sutta 95
Cynics 10–12, 16, 26, 55, 61
Cyrenaics 10–11, 15–16, 26, 39
Cyrus the Great 4

daemon 49
Darius I 4
Dedicatory Verses 100
Delphi 52
Democritus 4, 12–14, 17, 26, 104
denial of judgment 59–60
dependent origination 74
Descartes, R. 76
dhamma 70–1
dharmas 9, 78–86, 94
dialectics 52
dilemma 59, 93, 96
Diogenes 2–3, 9, 11–12, 21–33
dogmas 35
Dogmatism/Dogmatists 13, 36–8,
   43–7, 49, 60, 63, 65, 72–5, 78, 81,
   84, 87, 89–90, 96, 98–101
doxai 58
dualisms 100
duhkha 9
dukkha 8, 71

Eight-Fold Path 70
Eleusinian Mysteries 24
Empedocles 24
emptiness 66, 92–101; absence as
   Pyrrhonian equivalent of 97

enlightenment 25
Ephectics 26
Epicureanism/Epicureans 10,
   35–6, 49
Epicurus 22
Eternalism/Eternalists 65–6, 72–5, 81,
   87, 89
Euclid 10, 84
Eudoxus 4
Eurylochus 23
Eusebius 57
euthymia 13, 26
experiences 42

Favorinus 62
Fifth Postulate 84
First Turning 66–70, 73–4, 81, 87, 90,
   93–4, 97, 103, 105
Flintoff, E. 1
Four Noble Truths 67–8, 70

Garfield, J. 67
Gethin, R. 2
grāhakatva 110
grāhyatva 110
*Greek Buddha: Pyrrho's Encounter
   with Early Buddhism* (Beckwith) 7
gymnosophists 3–6, 9, 16, 22,
   35, 103–4

Halkias, G. 4–6
Heart Sutra 93
Hecataeus 23
Heiddeger, M. 55
hīnayāna 67
holy men 3–4, 18, 24–5
holy women 24
Hume, D. 44, 92
Husserl, E. 55–6, 86

Idea of History (Collingwood) 17
immortal men 87–8
indicative signs 47–8
intentio 56

James, W. 55
Jesus 24, 89, 107
jnanas 25
John the Baptist 24
Johnson, M.R. 13

Jones, H.S. 8
judgment, suspension of 48–9

Kaccana 71
Kaccānagotta 70–1
Kalanos 5, 62
karma 29
Kochumuttom, Thomas A. 109–10
kṣaṇa 80

lemma 59
Leucippus 14
Lexicon (Liddell/Scott) 77
Liddell, H.G. 8, 77
Lives of Eminent Philosophers (Diogenes) 21–2
Long, A.A. 57–8
Lucius Calvenus Tarsus 61–2
Lusthaus, D. 68, 86
Lycurgus 4

Madhyamaka 2, 6, 84
Madhyamaka and Pyrrhonism (Neale) 6
māhāyana 2, 67
Majjhima Nikaya 95
McEvilley, T. 12
meditation 103, 25
Megarians 10–11, 52, 54
Megarics 54
Merleau-Ponty, M. 55
mermaids 28
Methodism 46
Methodists 80
Middle Path 65, 71, 73, 84, 94
Middle Way school 68
Mind-Only school 68
modes 30–1
mokṣa 110
Monimus 55
mukti 110
Mulamadhyamakakarika 100

Nagarjuna 68, 99–100
nāma-rūpa 89
name-and-form 89
Neale, M. 4, 6–7
negative beliefs 69, 99
neurosis 96
Nietzsche, F.W. 1, 84
nirvana 35, 69, 94, 102, 108

nooumena 38
normative Buddhism 7–9, 72, 78, 83–4, 102
noumena 38

Olympic Games 62
Onesicritus 4, 10
Outlines of Pyrrhonism (Sextus Empiricus) 21, 36, 39, 43–4, 87
Outlines of Scepticism 101

Pali 66
Pali Canon 77–8
Pausanias 22
Peregrinus Proteus 61–2
Perfection of Wisdom 93
Perfection of Wisdom Sūtras 68
phainomena 38
phenomena 38, 73, 94
phenomenalistic atoms 15
phenomenology 55
Pistokrates 22
Piṭakas 66
Platonists 35
Plotinus 24
positive beliefs 38, 69, 99
positive dogmatism 89
pragma 59
pragmata 8–9, 13, 15, 26–7, 29, 39, 42, 47–8, 50, 54–5, 57–8, 65–90, 92–4, 96, 98–9, 106
prajñāpāramitā sūtras 93
pratītya-samutpāda 69, 81
pseudo-objects 89
psychosis 96
Ptolemy Philadelphus 53
Pudgalavādins 92
Pyrrho 1–4, 6–14; Alexander the Great's expedition 22; as a Buddhist *Arhat* 1; Diogenes on 21–7, 103–4; encounters with the *gymnosophists* in India 16, 18; Gellius on 62; reactions to experiences 24; Sextus Empiricus on 35–7; solitude 49; Timon on 52–4, 57; as yogi 24
Pyrrhonian Buddhism 3, 9, 14, 16, 59, 66, 78–80, 83, 86–9, 92, 94, 109
Pyrrhonian principle 31–2
Pyrrhonian Principles (Favorinus) 62

120 Index

Pyrrhonians 26–7, 55
Pyrrhonism 14, 35–6, 46, 49, 96; and Buddhism 1–3; four-fold logic of quadrilemma 59–60; phenomenalistic ontology of 43; sources of 21; versus Western philosophy 16
Pyrrhonism: How the Ancient Greeks Reinvented Buddhism 1–2, 4
Pyrrhonists 26–31, 37, 43, 49–50, 55–6, 62–3, 77, 87, 92, 103
Pythagoras 4, 24
Pythia 24
Pytho (Timon) 52

quadrilemma 59, 104

Reddoch, M.J. 16
Right View 72, 79

Sabbasava Sutta 95
Sakyamuni 7
samadi 25
samatha 25
Saṃdhinirmocana Sūtra 67, 105–6
sammā diṭṭhi 72
saṃsara 69
Saṃyutta Nikāya 70–1, 76
sanghas 5
saṅkhāra 76
Santa Claus 32, 98, 105–7
Sartre, J.P. 55
Sautrantikas 87
Sceptic 40
Sceptical Treatises (Sextus Empiricus) 36
scepticism 87
Sceptics 26
Schulman, E. 25
Scott, R. 8, 77
Scylax 4
Second Turning 66–70, 92–4, 96–7, 99, 103–5
self-immolation 61–2
sensory experiences 28–9
Sextus Empiricus 2–3, 6, 35–50; on Cyrenaics 11; on Democritus 13; on dogmatists 96; *Against the Learned* (or *Professors*) 36, 40–1;

Against the Logicians 43–8; modes 30; *Outlines of Pyrrhonism* 21; *Outlines of Scepticism* 41; on *pragmata* 77, 89; *Sceptical Treatises* 36; on skepticism 87–8
The Shape of Ancient Thought (McEvilley) 12
Shorter Instructions to Malunka 95
Shults, B. 13
Siderits, M. 81–2
skandhas 78, 84
Smith, D.W. 55
social signification 47
Socrates 10, 12, 24, 37, 41, 49, 52
Solon 4
sramanas 5–6, 9, 16, 18, 21
Stanford Encyclopedia of Philosophy 81
Stcherbatsky, T. 72, 80, 82
Stilpo 10–11, 52
Stoicism/Stoics 35–6, 49
Stoics 35
śūnyatā 93–4
suspension of belief 92–101
suspension of judgment 59–60, 66, 88
Sutta Piaka 71
suttas 71
svabhāva 93–4
Symposium (Plato) 49

Taints 95
tertium quid 1, 3, 65
The Will to Power (Nietzsche) 1
Theravadan Pali scriptures 93
Third Turning 67–70, 102–6
Three Doors of Liberation 7
Three Turnings of the Wheel of Dhama 66–9
Timon of Phlius 52–60; apprenticeship with Pyrrho 53; Aristocles passage 3, 8–9, 21, 57, 65; development into yogi 53; encounter with Pyrrho 52; Pyrrhonism in terms of the four-fold logic of the quadrilemma 59–60; settlement in Athens 53
tranquility 59–60
Treatise of the Three Natures 107
Trilaksana (Three Characteristics) 9

trilemma 59, 93, 96, 104
Tripitaka (three baskets) 2

unanswered questions 95, 100
unicorns 28
Urstad, K. 10

vajrayāna 67
Vico, Giambattista 17
vipassana 25
virtue 11

volutional formations 76

Yavanas 4
Yogacara 2, 67, 84, 103, 105, 109
yogi 24
Yonas 4

Zetetics 26
Zoroastrianism 8

For Product Safety Concerns and Information please contact our EU representative GPSR@taylorandfrancis.com
Taylor & Francis Verlag GmbH, Kaufingerstraße 24, 80331 München, Germany

www.ingramcontent.com/pod-product-compliance
Lightning Source LLC
Chambersburg PA
CBHW051754230426
43670CB00012B/2281